PEOPLE HIRE
PEOPLE
-Not Resumes

Written by

FRANK V. DANZO

"Frank brought in the concept and the system and I utilized it and it worked for me. I never really networked or made an attempt to network until I met Frank. The Career Networking system is a structured process, very results oriented if you follow the system."

Sheliah Thompson

"Frank provides a system to get in front of the decision makers."

Matt Drumm

"The Career Networking system is a way to take the responsibility of finding your next position into your own hands, as opposed to sending resumes over the Internet or passing resumes over the transom to the HR department. So it is definitely a system that allows you to take control and allows you to be as aggressive as you want in your job search."

Walter Bilgram

"Frank's advice and the way he dealt with me, and I presume other people, was so impressive. He asked good questions, listens to your answers and he responds to you with your specific needs."

Barry Murov

PEOPLE HIRE PEOPLE

-Not Resumes

Book edited by Murphy O'Brien
www.murphsturf.com

Assisted by Jennifer Danzo

Book design by Leslie Hinton
sheBang! design
www.shebangdesign.net

Cover photo: © Ian Hilliard. Image from BigStockPhoto.com

MPS Publishing
12977 North Forty Drive
Suite 100
St. Louis, MO 63141

ISBN 978-0-615-18111-0

PRINTED AND BOUND IN THE
UNITED STATES OF AMERICA
This book is printed on acid-free paper.

PEOPLE HIRE PEOPLE
-Not Resumes

Acknowledgements

There are a number of special people who have had a major impact on my life. Without their support and advice, my job search would have been much harder, and I wouldn't have had the courage to follow my heart and take the risks required to start coaching and write this book. Most importantly, my life is richer because they are part of it.

Lendell Phelps – My good friend Lendell has, and will always be, a role model for me. He'll never truly understand the positive influence he has had on me each day of my life.

Joe Castellano – Joe taught me to expand my perspective and see the best in people, even in difficult times. Joe is one of the *truly* good people in the world. What a privilege to know him so well.

Michael Bernardi – Michael has never given up on me. He has a way of increasing my self-confidence every time we talk.

Joe Ambrose – During my search Joe was always by my side, looking for opportunities to be of assistance. I am a better person because of his friendship.

Glenda Burch – Glenda's encouragement and faith in God gave me strength during my job search, and she continues to be a source of strength for me today.

Maura Lem – Without her persistence and encouragement, this book would never have been started or finished.

Brian Marchant-Calsyn – He believed in me more than I did. Thank you.

My parents – Always in my corner providing me with love and support. What great role models they have been for me throughout my life.

My girls - Jennifer, Kirsten, and Megan – The three people I adore most in life. They never question me, always providing unconditional love and affection. They taught me to judge people not by their income or job title, but by the difference they make in other peoples' lives. What a great lesson to learn from such special people!

Kathy – She is my Superwoman! Her constant love and support helped rebuild my confidence. I'm thankful everyday that she is in my life.

I extend my gratitude to each person that has enriched my life.

PEOPLE HIRE PEOPLE
-Not Resumes

Contents

PEOPLE HIRE PEOPLE

-Not Resumes

Introduction

Have you ever heard of "the perfect job candidate"? This person possesses the exact skills and experiences that a job requires, and the hiring manager is waiting for this person to contact them and take the job.

In my experience, the perfect candidate is a well-worn myth. In every job transition that I've made, I have fit the basic requirements of the job, but the reason that I was seriously considered and ultimately offered the position was **because the hiring managers knew me personally**. PEOPLE HIRE PEOPLE *-Not Resumes* draws from the truth of my experiences: employers hire job candidates based on the complete person, not a resume. The only way that hiring managers can appreciate you as a complete person is by meeting with you in person, and the most effective method of meeting hiring managers face-to-face is networking.

Although I was taught this lesson early in my career, I didn't actually learn the lesson until I was asked to leave a company that I had faithfully served for over 20 years. Only then did I realize the importance of networking. Since that time, I've taught hundreds of people how to network, assisted them in developing their own networks and helped them succeed in making their own job transitions. The purpose of this book is to help you transition jobs via a proven, real-world system, while also sharing many of the tips that I've learned through my own experiences. The true measure of my success is how quickly you land and ultimately how strong your network is years from today. Networking is not a "find-a-job-today" effort. It is meeting people and developing relationships that stand the test of time.

When you've finished this book, you'll know how to conduct a successful job search or career change that will be under your control.

Together, we will take each step to:

- Hold yourself accountable to ensure your success
- Develop a Personal Marketing Plan to guide your search
- Make your resume stand out by passing the 30 second thumb test
- Identify, meet and develop relationships with people that can make a difference in your career and your life
- Make phone calls that will generate networking meetings
- Write letters that will generate networking meetings
- Make your networking meetings productive
- Present yourself as the most qualified candidate to hiring managers
- Take control of your career
- Build powerful relationships that will last a lifetime

Every person I've worked with has been successful because they followed this system. Take the system seriously: it works.

PEOPLE HIRE PEOPLE
-Not Resumes

My Story

It was mid-morning and I was sitting in a department meeting with human resources professionals from all over the country when I received an e-mail on my Blackberry. Like a good corporate soldier, I immediately popped it off my belt, and saw that the Vice President of Sales' Assistant needed me to call her. After excusing myself from the meeting, I called his assistant, who asked me to attend a 1:00 P.M. meeting in the Vice President's office. When I inquired about the topic of the meeting, she said she was unsure. I immediately called my boss to see if he could offer any insight. He told me that he was aware of the meeting; however, he would not be in attendance. In respect to the subject of the meeting, he commented that it concerned "your future with the company". At that point, I knew what was coming.

Six months earlier, my boss of seven years and several of his peers had traded positions. My new boss was irritated by the changes as he felt it took him out of the mainstream of the company and off course to become President. It was common knowledge he felt being President was the natural next step in his career. I knew it was just a matter of time before he would leave.

Three weeks before my call he had resigned and the

political wheels started spinning. It was time for a reorganization and when the dust settled, my job had been eliminated. Twenty years and two million air miles later, I was on the outside looking in. The next four months was the most hellish period of my life.

During that time, I wrote and rewrote my resume at least fifty times, applied for every job imaginable, and slipped into depression. I was out of control both personally and professionally. Fortunately for me, I had a great wife, career coach and doctor. One day, I was sitting at my desk at the outplacement office when my wife called. She said she had made a doctor's appointment for me later that morning. I told her I wasn't going; everything was fine. Just then, my career coach walked in and together they strong-armed me to go to the doctor.

When Dr. Saltman walked into the examination room, I broke down. Even though he now had a hysterical, middle-aged man on his hands, he was caring and patient with me. He took the time to listen and developed a plan to help me get my act together. As we prepared to leave the exam room, Dr. Saltman asked if my children had acted any differently toward me. I responded that they still loved me as always. He said that was because they knew that the true value of a person comes from the person, not their job, title or money. His wisdom continues to influence me to this day.

With the assistance from my wife, Kathy, and Dr. Saltman, I finally got my act together. Kathy and I discussed what was important in our lives and the type of job I'd be looking for. We agreed that we didn't want to relocate, since our oldest daughter was entering high school and we didn't want to disrupt her life. I knew this decision would limit my opportunities and make my search more difficult, but I was willing to take that risk for my family.

My former career at a Fortune 50 company had been very successful, and I thought that would be a huge selling point on my resume. My resume did open many doors, but whenever I spoke with people from other large corporations, they were more curious about what had happened than seriously interested in hiring me. I began to feel that instead of giving me a great head start, *my resume was actually preventing me from returning to the workforce.* I had made an important realization: a resume can be your worst enemy in a job search, and in most cases it's best if you avoid sharing your resume with potential employers for as long as possible.

During my job search, I considered nearly every possible option. I deliberated going to law school but after talking with friends that were attorneys I realized it would never pay off at my age. I talked to a franchise broker, looking for that perfect match. Kathy really thought I had gone crazy when I considered buying a day-care business; then she knew I was crazy when I visited a manufacturer of frozen Italian foods. But no matter how wide-ranging these options may have been, they proved valuable because they helped me eliminate the jobs I didn't want and clarified my vision of what I wanted to do.

Once I worked through these farfetched possibilities,

I became focused and truly began my job search. During this time, I connected with hundreds of people who were willing to meet and assist me in furthering my job search. Most of those who helped were total strangers and benefited little, if at all, from assisting me. As I continued my job search, I decided that once I found a job, I would create a way to assist others in my situation, or as a good friend put it, "pay forward" the investment others had made in me.

My career coach kept telling me that I had to "network" if I wanted to find my next job. That advice was dead on, but not very helpful because I had no idea what networking meant. My previous work life consisted of waking up at 4:30 A.M., spending up to 70% of my time traveling, and arriving home LATE. When I wasn't traveling or working, all I wanted to do was spend time with my family. I didn't invest time in meeting people outside of work, so I didn't have a network of contacts. Each week when I met with my career coach, her advice was to network, network, network. I eventually figured out what she meant, but I could never get answers to the questions, "What is networking?" or "How do you network?"

I'm still amazed by the network that led me to my next job. During my daughter's soccer game I explained my situation to Andy, whose daughter was also on the team. Andy had been through a transition, so he could relate to my situation. He asked for my resume and offered to circulate it through his company. I eagerly agreed.

After I e-mailed Andy my resume, I kept calling and

e-mailing to see if he had anyone willing to talk with me. Almost a month passed before Andy finally introduced me to Chip. I called Chip and he agreed to meet with me, but as we talked, I realized he was in the process of moving to St. Louis for the first time. As I hung up, I thought to myself, "What a waste of time! Chip is new to the company and city; he doesn't know anybody!" I nearly called back and cancelled.

I'm not sure why, but I kept the appointment. Chip was a great guy, but as I expected he didn't have any contacts in St. Louis yet. As we discussed the companies I was targeting, he said he knew someone who worked for BJC HealthCare. They had worked together in Washington, D. C. He said he would try to contact Leon and would get back to me if he had any luck. I left the meeting convinced that my instincts had been right; meeting with Chip was a waste of time.

Two days later, Chip forwarded an e-mail from Leon; she said she would be happy to assist me, and suggested I give her a call. When I called the next day, Leon referred me to a co-worker, Nancy, and suggested that the two of us meet. I called Nancy and set up a meeting with her, which went exceedingly well, and she graciously provided a number of referrals, including a co-worker who happened to be on my target list.

At Nancy's suggestion, I e-mailed her co-worker, Bob. We set up a time to talk on the phone, and after a brief discussion Bob asked me to join him and one of his direct reports, Jim, for lunch. We discussed my experiences as well as the challenges that they were currently facing as they built a new department. After

20 minutes, they told me about a new position they had in the works. We agreed that I was a good match for the position, and they suggested that I meet with Jim the next week to talk in more detail. It was at this meeting that I learned that the job description hadn't been written. I volunteered to draft the job description, which I hoped would accelerate the hiring process. After we revised the job description several times, Jim asked me to come in for a formal interview. The two of us talked for over an hour, and then I had a group interview with the rest of his department heads.

Two weeks later, Jim called to offer me the position. I had successfully networked my way to a new position! It was amazing that I had been able to find a position that had not previously existed or ever been advertised. Through my networking, I was crossing both industries (from consumer products to healthcare) and job functions (operations to construction management). Thus, I had finally learned the power of networking.

After I started the job, I began coaching individuals through their own job searches. I had a steady stream of people calling me and asking for advice. I've now worked one-on-one with over 100 individuals, and I'm proud that every pupil has worked hard and landed successfully.

Since I could only work one-on-one with a limited number of job seekers, I offered to join forces with a volunteer organization and conduct a networking workshop, thus expanding the number of people that we could assist. Since we started the workshop, I've trained over 1,000 people on the job search system that worked for me. The more people I worked with, the more I realized that this was what I wanted to do everyday as a profession. With the support of Brian Marchant-Calsyn, a highly successful entrepreneur, we founded Career Networking Pro. Now I spend my days assisting others as they transition from one employer to another; coaching people between jobs on how to accelerate their job search and find the job they want; advising currently employed people on ways to improve their performance; and advising businesses on how to gain new clients through the power of networking and referrals.

PEOPLE HIRE PEOPLE

-Not Resumes

Step 1: Preparing for Your Job Search

During your career, you've been involved in projects where success hinges on effective management. A job search is no different. Like a successful project, your job search process consists of distinct steps, such as setting objectives, establishing target dates, and implementing tools that track and measure progress. Together, we'll break your job search into small steps with specific activities you need to complete. It is important to follow each step in order, as each piece builds on its predecessor. The last chapter in the book is a set of job search tools to increase the effectiveness of your search. Use **Job Search Tool 1: Preparation Plan Checklist** (p145) to track the completion of each item in this section.

Successful projects are undertaken with specific objectives in mind. The first objective you need to identify is the number of hours per week you're going to invest in your job search. If you're between jobs, invest *at least* as much time into your search as you invested in your previous job. **Your job search is now your full-time job.**

Job Search Tool 2: Productivity Tracking Chart (p146) shows one method for tracking the time you're investing toward your objective. Track your time investment each day of your job search to stay focused, productive and motivated.

Daily Routine

It can be easy to fall out of a routine without the pressure of having to "go to work". Be careful to avoid soft, time-wasting habits like sleeping in or staying up late. Finding your next job *is* a full-time job; let your schedule reflect this responsibility.

Get up at the same time every day. Take a shower, get dressed, eat breakfast and "get to work" by an established time. If you have a networking meeting later in the day, get dressed as if you're going first thing. Dressing in jeans, then changing into business casual reduces your productivity. If you are always dressed to network, you're constantly prepared to meet with anyone when it is most convenient for them.

By creating a daily routine and dressing as if you're working at a formal job, you are preparing yourself mentally and physically for networking. In addition, it prevents you from forming bad work habits, which could foil you from landing your next job or being successful once you land.

Although you may feel like you have more free time now, don't spend all of your time running errands and doing odd jobs around the house. Let your family and friends know that a significant amount of time every day will be spent on your job search. However, it is perfectly alright to take advantage of your more flexible schedule, so long as you manage your time. You can still help out with your child's school activities or go out to lunch with your spouse or a friend. Just be sure that you manage your time and don't allow others to take control.

Your workday only ends once you've reached your objectives for that day. Give yourself small rewards for meeting daily objectives or reaching networking goals that we'll establish in Step 3: Constructing Your Networking Plan. Job search is hard work so read for pleasure, go to the gym, or see a movie. Keep your life in balance and celebrate your successes.

Office Set-up

If you'll be working from home, find a space that will be your "office". It should be a place where you can work uninterrupted, make private phone calls, and receive minimal distractions from family, pets, and the outdoors. You should be able to leave this place at the end of the day so that your mind gets a break from work as well.

If you have a friend that can provide an unused office, cubical or empty desk, take advantage of that opportunity. Having a place to physically go to and represent your "workplace" can be a great psychological boost.

Regardless of where your office is located, equipping your new office properly is an essential part of a productive search. Use **Job Search Tool 3: Office Checklist** (p147) to ensure that you have the necessary tools to start your job search. Additional tools and supplies may be necessary later, depending on the direction your search takes. Be creative in determining the best tools to support your job search.

Search Coach

The time spent transitioning between jobs is a challenge for job seekers and their families. A professional coach that you can turn to for support and advice is critical to your job search. Your spouse cannot fill this role due to a lack of objectivity, as they're as emotionally vested as you are. Engage a professional coach or ask a good friend, relative, or business associate to act in this role for you. Having someone to act as a sounding board and hold you accountable to achieve your objectives will reduce the time it takes for you to land.

Here are important traits that your search coach should possess:

- ✓ They must be someone that you highly respect and will listen to.
- ✓ They must be willing to be brutally honest. It is better to hear the truth from them than wonder why your search stretches on.
- ✓ They must be a great listener. This provides a safe environment for you to vent and share your thoughts.
- ✓ They must be persistent and driven to keep you focused and accountable for achieving your objectives.

It's also beneficial if your search coach has conducted their own job search. The experience and knowledge they gained in their search will allow them to better help you.

The role of the search coach is to keep you focused on the job search process, serve as a sounding board for ideas, provide support during challenging times, and hold you accountable to achieve the goals you committed to. Schedule a regular day, time, and place to meet with your coach. While preparing for your job search, it's most beneficial if you meet weekly so that you can receive feedback and learn as much as possible about the job search process. After you start executing your plan, meet every other week and follow up with phone calls and e-mails between meetings. Your coach's constant positive influence will increase your productivity and decrease the length of your search.

Support Chain

When you're dealing with the loss of a job, don't feel ashamed. Remind yourself that you aren't the only person that has gone through this process. In fact, many of the people that you'll network with have been in similar situations. During my job search nearly half the people that assisted me had been through their own transition. In today's world of mergers, buyouts, down-sizing, right-sizing, etc., finding yourself in search of a new job is rather common.

A job search can be an emotional rollercoaster, so it's incredibly important that you don't isolate yourself. Boost your spirits by spending more time with family and friends.

This is also a good time to create a Support Chain, a list of close family and friends. When you invite someone to be in your Support Chain, it's important that you clearly explain why you have chosen them and how they can help you. Here are some examples:

- Encourage you to stay positive and upbeat
- Ensure you're presenting yourself positively
- Listen and offer support
- Provide advice on your plans
- Act as a practice partner for networking meetings
- Act as a practice partner for interviews
- Provide networking contacts
- Provide input on your resume and cover letters

Once you've created the list, call each person. Let them know your situation and ask if you'll be able to count on their support. Confirm their preferred phone number so that you know the best way to contact them when you need assistance or want to provide an update on your job search and agree to the frequency that you will touch base with them. You should have as many supporters as possible to ensure that you'll be able to reach someone whenever you need to. Remember, no one person can possibly be available at all times. If you can't contact one supporter or they're unable to provide help, try the next person in your Support Chain.

Motivations and Rewards

Human nature causes each of us to be motivated by different things. During my job search my personal motivation came from my kids. I kept a picture of them next to the phone, and each time I felt weak or unmotivated, I would look at the picture and it would give me the strength to pick up the phone and make the next call. Your motivation may be your family, your next vacation, or the next challenge in your career. Make a list of things that motivate you and select one.

Keep this image in highly visible places where you'll see it each day, such as beside the phone, on your desk, and in your car.

Identify specific, short-term activities that you find enjoyable and use them as rewards. For instance, I love taking walks with my wife. My reward for a hard day's work was an evening walk where she'd recount her day and I'd share mine. For you, it may be going to the gym, indulging in your favorite hobby, or reading a magazine. Whenever you accomplish a goal, review your list of rewards, pick one and remember to reward yourself. Job search is hard work, so celebrate your successes.

Recommended Readings

One of the most difficult challenges a person can face is the inability to control changes within their own life. Most people fear what they can't control, and are often allergic to change; they prefer the stability and familiarity of known quantities. That's why I recommend reading *"Who Moved My Cheese?"* by Spencer Johnson, a short, easy-to-read book that will help you keep change in perspective. Every year I read this book to prepare myself for the unforeseen changes around each and every corner.

Staying abreast of current events within the business world, your specific industry, and the local community is even more important as you transition jobs. Your reading selection should include daily local newspapers, local business publications, The Wall Street Journal, magazines, and newsletters focused on your industry, profession, or community. Make a list of the publications you need to read, the source of the publication, and how frequently it is published. Keep this in a convenient place to remind yourself to read them. Many of these resources can be found online or at the local public library. Take a break from making phone calls or between networking meetings by reading these periodicals at the library, rather than footing the subscription bill and reading them at home.

Contact Information

Your phone number and e-mail address will become the most critical information in your job search. You need to present networking contacts with contact information that will stay consistent both during your job search AND once your job search is completed. This consistency will ensure that you don't miss out on a job or networking opportunity, and also showcases your reliability and stability as a potential referral now and in the future.

If you're using a temporary office, don't use the temporary phone number. If you're unsure if you will have a mobile phone throughout your entire job search, then avoid that number. It's better to use your home number, rather than take the risk that someone will be unable to reach you. Use the consistent phone number on your business card, resume, Networking Plan, e-mails and all correspondence. If you have two consistent phone numbers, list the preferred number first on each communication tool.

If you don't have a personal e-mail address, it's essential that you create one. You can sign up for a free e-mail address from Yahoo or your Internet provider. Keep your e-mail address simple, descriptive and professional. Place your last name within your e-mail address so those receiving your e-mails can easily identify the sender. This will help prevent people from mistakenly deleting your e-mails, as they will be more easily distinguished from junk mail. Nicknames, letter combinations and numbers are generally a bad idea. A short address is better because it's easy for the recipient to recognize.

Stick with a simple, memorable e-mail address, and you'll make the networking process much easier for you and your contacts.

Business Cards

A business card is a **requirement** for any job search. When you offer your card to a contact, you're presenting yourself as a professional and a person of substance. Exchanging business cards also enables you to politely solicit their contact information.

A high-quality business card is certainly worth the investment. When you give your card to someone, they may keep it for years, and it will serve as a reflection of your worth. If you use cheap paper and poor quality printing, it will become torn and faded, so that you're no longer the problem-solver with great experience, but rather a decent prospect with a cheap business card. A durable, high-quality card makes for a better impression and improves the chance of people keeping it and using it in the future.

As you design your business card, keep the information

simple and professional. Avoid gimmicks such as quotes or clip art that could distract potential contacts. The focus of your business card is your name, so make sure it draws attention with a large, legible bolded font. Include your primary phone number, personal e-mail address and mailing address. Put your phone number and e-mail address above your mailing address, establishing a hierarchy that prioritizes phone or e-mail as the best way to contact you. A number of clients have had concerns about providing so much personal information, especially their home address. If this is a concern for you, it is perfectly acceptable to delete your home address and only include your phone number and e-mail address.

If you have a professional expertise such as Certified Public Accountant (CPA) that you want to communicate, include this on your business card next to or below your name. Any certification or license that distinguishes you and supports your job search should also be included. These credentials successfully communicate that you are more qualified for certain positions than those without this professional expertise.

When you're ready to print, go to a local printer, copy store or rely on a web-based printer such as VistaPrint to compare quality and price. If you have a high-quality printer, consider printing your own cards. Choose a premium paper such as linen or laid. The paper should have a texture to it, rather than feeling slick, so that it feels solid and substantial. Request that the print be raised so it also has a "feel" to it. This is more expensive, but will provide the professional image you want. You should purchase between 500 and 1000 cards, which may seem like a lot right now, but you'll be using more and more of them as your network grows.

Thank You Notes

Thank you notes will help make you more memorable during your job search. Keep in mind that you are trying to build a relationship with people. To do this you need to be remembered. Sending a handwritten thank you note after meeting someone will give you a more personal, professional image than an e-mail or typed letter. Such a gesture demonstrates that you care enough to invest time in the relationship.

It's best to buy small, simple, and professional note cards. Smaller note cards limit the amount of space in which to write, allowing you to be brief and to the point. When purchasing your note cards, keep in mind that you will need one thank you card for each person you meet. Your local dollar store will have cards to meet your need at the best price.

Keep Your Life in Balance

A balanced lifestyle is critical before, during, and after a job transition. It's very important that you take care of yourself both physically and mentally during this emotional time to lower the risk of burnout, high anxiety, or depression. While these emotions are somewhat expected and natural, if you don't manage them correctly, they can dangerously tamper with the success of your job search.

Set aside time within your daily routine for physical activity, such as walking or riding an exercise bike. This will help reduce nervous energy and increase your positive energy level, as well as maintaining your overall health. Eating healthy is equally as important. Be wary of bad diets or snacking all the time. Good physical health is a boon for your psyche, and will make your job search more productive.

It's also important to stimulate your mind with thoughts other than your job search. Set aside time each day to take a break from your work, and exercise your brain in other fun and rewarding ways. Read a book, play chess, or do a crossword puzzle. This will keep your brain challenged and healthy!

You'll land that job; just follow these steps and you'll have an easier time of it.

PEOPLE HIRE PEOPLE
-Not Resumes

Step 2: Marketing Yourself

Companies spend millions of dollars creating and executing marketing plans because they know their initial investment will pay off in higher sales. In all likelihood, you don't have millions of dollars to market yourself, but neither do your competitors. If you want to have an edge over your competitors, you're going to need something they don't have: a Marketing Plan.

A Marketing Plan is the key to successfully selling yourself to new contacts and potential employers. Invest the time to develop a great Marketing Plan, and you'll be fully prepared to promote yourself.

Your Marketing Plan will be your road map to your next job, providing clarity and focus for your job search. An excellent plan can be the difference between a slow, wandering search and a rapid, strategic search. It will help you find the sweet spot between what you want to do, what you are qualified to do, and what someone will pay you to do.

Use **Job Search Tool 4: Marketing Plan Checklist** (p148) to track the completion of each item in this chapter.

Productivity Tracking

Continue to track the number of hours you invest in your job search per week using **Job Search Tool 2: Productivity Tracking Chart** (p146). At the very least, you should continue to invest as much time on your job search as you did in your last position. Tracking your investment throughout your job search will keep you focused, productive, and motivated.

Transitioning Message

During your job search, whether you're working or not, people will wonder and ask: Why are you looking for a job? Your Transitioning Message should clearly answer this question with the utmost brevity. Follow these guidelines for constructing your Transitioning Message:

1. Be brief (one or two sentences).
2. Be factual.
3. Don't sound defensive or make excuses about your situation.
4. Don't be negative about your current or previous employer.
5. Be optimistic and focused on the future.

Job Search Tool 5: Transitioning Message (p149) provides examples of Transitioning Messages.

A quick tip: type out your Transitioning Message to ensure that you invest the necessary time and care. By forcing yourself to write it out, the end product will be substantially improved. When you're done, read your message out loud so you can listen to the delivery and ask yourself these questions:

- Do the words flow naturally?
- Am I using words I normally use when I speak?
- Is the message factual?
- Is the message positive?
- Is the message as brief as it can be?
- Does the message cause additional questions?

Practice reading your Transitioning Message aloud until it becomes natural, and then continue until you've memorized it. This practice will reduce your anxiety when people ask why you're looking for a job. When you're satisfied with your Transitioning Message, test it out on your career coach and your Support Chain. Ask for feedback on the message content and your delivery, and then use their feedback to finalize your message. Keep a copy on your desk to use while making phone calls, and place a copy in your car to review before networking meetings or interviews.

As a general rule, don't share your Transitioning Message with people unless asked. You want your conversations focused on the future, not the past. Likewise, avoid additional comments or prolonged pauses after sharing your Transitioning Message, as this will only focus the dialogue on the past. If you're asked about your job search, share your Transitioning Message and immediately shift the conversation to another topic. This can be done by asking an open-ended question or sharing your Personal Marketing Story, which we will develop later in this chapter.

Now that we've developed the message of why you're seeking a new job, let's define the package you are selling. We'll do this by identifying your Transferable

Skills, Personal Characteristics, and Accomplishment Stories which we will craft into your Personal Marketing Story.

Transferable Skills

Skills are defined as abilities learned and acquired through training. Developing a list of your skills will prepare you to sell yourself to a new employer, focus your search on positions that require your skills, and provide long-term job satisfaction.

Take a look at **Job Search Tool 6: Transferable Skills** (p150) to identify the skills that you can market to a new employer. The Transferable Skills List is divided into five categories: communications, people, thinking, organizing, and function. Select each skill and function where you feel you have an expertise. This list is just a sample, so add additional skills or functions that create an accurate picture of you. Put the list down and come back to it later. This will give you time to let your selections sink in.

Next, narrow your function to two or three options. The more specific you can be about your function, the easier it will be to identify potential opportunities. Then refine your skills selections to a maximum of 10 from the other four categories, with at least one from each category. Again, put the list aside to give yourself time to let your selections sink in.

Look at the list of skills you've identified and underline or highlight your top four skills along with your preferred job function. This combination is unique to you and will assist in distinguishing you from other candidates.

You'll rely on these skills and function to craft your Personal Marketing Story.

Personal Characteristics

Characteristics are defined as distinguishing traits and qualities. Examine **Job Search Tool 7: Personal Characteristics** (p151) to identify the Personal Characteristics that best describe you. It is best if the final words you use can be attributed to someone other than you such as a past boss, performance review, 360-degree survey, or co-workers. Potential employers are more interested in what other people think of you than what you think of yourself.

The Personal Characteristic List is divided into four categories: personal style, attitude, interpersonal style, and work habits. Select each characteristic which an objective third party has described you as. The list is just a sample so add additional characteristics that create an accurate picture of you. Put the list down and come back to it later.

Narrow your selection to a maximum of 10 characteristics, with at least two from each category. Again, put the list aside to give yourself time to let your selections sink in.

Look at the list of characteristics you've identified and underline or highlight your top four characteristics. Your unique combination of characteristics will help hiring managers distinguish you from other candidates. You'll rely on these characteristics to build your Personal Marketing Story.

Collectively, your transferable skills and personal characteristics are the features of the product you are selling...YOU! Next, we will identify your product benefits or your accomplishments.

Accomplishment Statements

When writing your Accomplishment Statements, invest more time and effort in those achieved during the past seven to ten years. These will be most applicable to a new employer. Accomplishment Statements should be quantifiable, action-oriented, and clearly demonstrate the value you added in the position.

Consider the following questions when drafting your Accomplishment Statements:

1. What were the results of a problem you solved?
2. Did you introduce a new system that made a process more efficient or accurate? How much was the process improved?
3. Did you save the company money? How much?
4. Did you increase sales? How much?
5. Did you increase profits? How much?
6. Did you increase margins? How much?
7. Did you manage people or systems? How many? How did they improve?
8. Did you initiate a new sales program? What was the increase in sales?
9. Did you plan and execute a project? What was the benefit to the company?
10. Did you prepare special reports or publications? What was the benefit to the reader? Who were the readers? Did the number of readers increase?
11. How much did you improve efficiencies?

12. How much did you increase production capacit,
13. Were you involved in a start-up or shut down? What was your impact?
14. Did you automate processes? What was the benefit to the company?
15. Did you receive any special awards? What accomplishment was recognized?

For your resume, write your Accomplishment Statements in the Results - Action format. First, state the results you achieved; then outline specific actions that led to those results.

The following Accomplishment Statements exemplify the Results - Action format.

RESULTS
Increased client base 25% in less than one year

ACTION
by developing and implementing a new
sales strategy.

RESULTS
Improved daily output by 2,000 units or 20%

ACTION
by redesigning production line work flow.

You should use a variety of sentence starters to make your Accomplishment Statements more powerful. Begin each statement with power verbs such as "increased," "improved," "reduced," "grew," "initiated," "led," "planned," or "implemented". Review **Job Search**

Tool 8: Accomplishment Power Verbs (p152) for suggested sentence starters.

The golden rule of writing an accomplishment is to quantify the impact with numbers. Numbers speak loudly on a resume because they make your accomplishments concrete and easily understood. You don't need to provide the full story; provide just enough information so that the reader wants to learn more by talking with you directly.

Every time you say that you improved something, increased sales or reduced costs, quantify the amount. If you don't have the data to accurately calculate the impact, then develop a reasonable estimate. Write out all the assumptions necessary to estimate your impact. By writing them out it will force you to question the reasonableness of each assumption. "Reasonable" means saying you increased sales by 8%, when you estimate the impact was between 7% and 9% (not between 5% and 8%). It's reasonable to say you saved the company $250,000 when you estimate the impact to be between $240,000 and $260,000 (not between $230,000 and $250,000).

The ultimate test for each estimate is the "Look in the Mirror" test. Can you look yourself in the mirror, say the accomplishment out loud, and believe that your estimate is as accurate and reasonable as possible? The goal here isn't to be deceptive (if a prospective employer does their fact-checking, any inconsistencies will come to light); rather, it's to be as truthful, authentic, and powerful as possible. You can't betray an ounce of doubt when presenting your accomplishments; a credible and trustworthy image is critical to building a relationship, especially one that's just begun.

Now you're ready to draft your Accomplishment Statements. Write your statements (from your former employer's viewpoint) for each position held at that organization. Start with your greatest accomplishment, the one of which you are most proud, and work backward. Include even the smallest accomplishment; it may seem small to you but could have a very large impact on a prospective employer.

Write your Accomplishment Statements for every organization you've worked for and every position you've held. Later you'll pick the strongest statements to include in your resume.

Accomplishment Stories

Now that you have completed your Accomplishment Statements, select the one accomplishment that you are most proud of and write an Accomplishment Story. We write stories to ensure we select the best combination of words and phrases to describe our impact. Our stories will be shared verbally so choose words you speak rather than words you write.

Accomplishment Stories are written in the reverse order as Accomplishment Statements with detail added. First, tell the listener the situation, outlining the problem to solve or objective to achieve. Then summarize the solution implemented and give enough detail for the listener to clearly understand your contribution. Finally, complete the story by reviewing the results.

Follow the STAR format to craft each of your stories.

ST (situation) - Provide an overview of the situation that led to your actions. What was the opportunity or problem to be solved?

A (action)   - Describe the specific actions you took to capitalize on the opportunity or solve the problem.

R (results) - Quantify the results achieved by your efforts. Numbers speak louder than words.

As an example, the Accomplishment Statement in your resume would be written as:

Expanded client base by 25% in less than one year by developing and implementing a new sales strategy.

When a prospective employer asks about the accomplishment on your resume, you should share your Accomplishment Story:

The client base between Sales Representatives varied widely, and all Sales Representatives didn't aggressively pursue new clients. We analyzed client bases by Sales Territory identifying which territories had the largest opportunity for growth. Working with the Territory Sales Managers and Sales Representatives, we developed plans that identified targeted clients, clarified responsibilities, and set specific goals. Variable compensation for the Sales Representatives was tied directly to the achievement of these specific goals. Monthly meetings were held with each Sales Representative to review progress, providing coaching for success and modify plans. In the first year, the overall client base increased by over 25%, with territory increases as high as 50%.

Type your Accomplishment Story so that you invest the necessary thought to make it specific, quantifiable, and compelling. When you're done, read the story aloud, listen to the delivery, and ask yourself these questions.

- Do the words flow naturally?
- Am I using words I normally use when I speak?
- Have I explained the situation clearly enough so the listener understands the problem we were trying to solve?
- Have I provided enough detail in the action taken so the listener understands my contribution?
- Have I quantified the results?

We will use this Accomplishment Story in your Personal Marketing Story.

Personal Marketing Story

Your Personal Marketing Story is an opportunity to answer the key question that you'll be asked throughout your job search:

"What do you want to do?"

By sharing your Personal Marketing Story with contacts, you can start shaping their mental image of you and clearly define how they can assist you best. Job search, especially networking, is primarily a verbal communication process, so keep the message simple.

Impress a listener with your story and they'll want to learn more about you and share your story with others. Your Personal Marketing Story is the launching pad for future dialogues.

A Personal Marketing Story focuses and gives direction to your search by clarifying exactly what you're seeking and clearly communicating that goal to others. As you write your story, use words that you want others to use to describe you. Minimize the labels you place on yourself as this sets an artificial boundary which you and your contacts will not cross.

As an example, I see many mid-level managers label themselves "senior executive." The problem with this label is that the definition of "senior executive" varies greatly across companies. I often ask clients whether they would accept a Director-level position if the compensation was within their expectations. Most say yes, but when I ask if they consider a Director-level position to be a "senior executive" job, they say no. Don't put a label on yourself that could exclude you from a position you would accept. The clearer and more focused you can be, the shorter your job search will be.

Your Personal Marketing Story should be under one minute in length so that the message is clear and easy for the listener to remember. Your Personal Marketing Story should include:

Features
- Transferable Skills – your strengths
- Personal Characteristics – as described by others

Benefits
- Accomplishment Story – your proudest achievement

Focus
- Type of job you are looking for

Review **Job Search Tool 9: Personal Marketing Story** (p153) for an example of a client's Personal Marketing Story.

Now it's time to construct your Personal Marketing Story. Use the features you identified as your top Transferable Skills and Personal Characteristics to describe yourself, as well as your most impressive benefit or Accomplishment Story.

After you've written your Personal Marketing Story, read it aloud and listen to make sure it sounds natural. Read it to your career coach and Support Chain and ask for feedback to finalize your Personal Marketing Story. When you make phone calls, keep a copy in front of you as a fail-safe until you have it memorized. It's also valuable to review your Personal Marketing Story before a networking meeting to make sure your delivery is consistent and sincere.

At the beginning of your job search, it's okay to have more than one Personal Marketing Story. You can use these initial networking meetings as a test market, but be certain to only use one message per meeting. Ask for feedback on how your Personal Marketing Story fits your background and sharpen your focus to one message as quickly as possible. A sharp, accurate Personal Marketing Story will help you stand out and accelerate the search process.

Your Personal Marketing Story should be included in your Networking Plan (which we'll construct in the Step 3: Constructing Your Networking Plan) and can be used in your phone scripts, resume, cover letters, and any other communication vehicle.

Since networking is a verbal communication process, getting others to pass along your information is vital to your success. This is why your Personal Marketing Story is so important. The clearer and simpler your Personal Marketing Story, the easier it is for others to share with their contacts.

Target People and Companies
Target people are:
- employees at your target companies that have the authority to hire you
- people who can introduce you to a person that can hire you
- people that can introduce you to new people to expand your Circle of Contacts

Similarly, target companies are:
- companies that you are interested in working for
- companies that have a need for your skills
- companies that you want to learn more about as a potential employer

There are two objectives when developing a Target List of people and companies. First, to focus your search on companies you have an interest in working for. Second, to educate those you will be meeting with on how to best assist you in your networking.

Your goal is to identify as many companies as possible that you have interest in and then find the people in those organizations that are in a position to hire you. Start a list of people that you want to network with, whether you know them personally or not. Include their name, office phone number, mobile number, e-mail address, company, and title. Complete the information you know and your networking will uncover the rest.

Start a list of target companies you want to explore and learn more about. Fill this document with your competitors, suppliers, customers, and other companies that you're aware of and would like to learn more about. You can find prospective target companies in resources such as Sorkin's Directory, Dun and Bradstreet, local business journals, and a listing of licensed businesses in your target city or cities. This list is public information and most cities only charge the cost of copying. Visit your city hall and asked the city clerks office for the information. Your local public library is another great resource. Visit the reference section and ask them for assistance in identifying potential companies.

Internet research companies such as Strategic Research Network (SRN) offer services to develop customized lists of companies and contacts within those companies for a reasonable fee. To learn more about these services, visit their website at www.strategicresearchnetwork.com

Resume

Your resume is your sales brochure, and YOU are the

product you're selling. The purpose of the resume is to support your efforts to market yourself and provide tangible, real world benefits that exemplify the value of your skills and experiences. Your resume should provide just enough information to stimulate the reader's curiosity so they want to meet and learn more about you in person.

No one can write your resume better than you can. Don't rely on a resume service or a well-meaning friend. When someone else writes your resume it ends up including words and phrases that aren't natural for you. You should rely on an editor and someone with a critical eye to provide feedback on your grammar, formatting, and wording, but you must own the document. It's this combination that will make your resume unique to you and stand out.

Most hiring authorities prefer a chronological resume, which places emphasis on your most recent job experience. If you have a specialty/expertise which confines you to a particular industry, limited employers or recent gaps in your resume, then consider using a functional resume, which lists your experience and accomplishments by skills rather than employer. Avoid this format if possible.

Before starting your resume, find an example that provides the "look" you like. Review resumes you've collected and search the Internet for examples, then use the best example as the blueprint for constructing your resume. Review **Job Search Tool 10: Resume Guidelines** (p154-156) for additional suggestions as you construct your resume.

Resume Guidelines

- The top half of the first page is the most impo[rtant] real estate; invest more time in this section to give it the most impact.
- Limit the resume to two pages. Focus on your most recent experience, and if necessary, only list job titles and dates for positions you held over 10 years ago.
- Do not use odd-sized paper, colors, style, or fonts. A resume should look like a resume.
- Ask at least two other people (one person from your industry, and another with expertise in English or Journalism) to review your resume for clarity, understanding, and mistakes such as typos, spelling, grammar, or syntax.

The 30 Second Thumb Test

Now that you've completed your resume, let's test it. *Remember, most decisions on resumes are made within 30 seconds or before finishing the first half page.* Take the first page of the resume and fold it in half. Now scan the top half of the page and ask yourself the following questions:

Are you the only person who could put their name at the top of this resume?

If the answer is no, then the resume is too generic and not unique enough to you.

Does the document catch your attention with action words, quantified accomplishments and crisp, clean presentation?

If the answer is no, then the resume isn't engaging enough to the reader.

Would you want to talk to this person to learn more about specific accomplishments or experiences?

If the answer is no, then the resume doesn't clearly display the value you bring to an organization.

If you passed, congratulations! Take a break and reward yourself for your hard work. If you didn't pass the 30 Second Thumb Test, ask your career coach for suggestions on how to improve the document.

Once you have completed your resume, write an Accomplishment Story for every Accomplishment Statement included in your resume. Sharing your stories will make your accomplishments more impactful and memorable. Prepare your stories now, review them before each meeting, and you'll be ready to share them while networking or interviewing.

Select two additional Accomplishment Statements from the last seven to 10 years. We will use these Accomplishment Statements in your Networking Plan, which we will develop in the next chapter.

View these Accomplishment Statements as your career headlines. By including the most impactful in your Personal Marketing Story, in your Networking Plan and highlighting them in your resume, you will guide people toward the accomplishments you're best prepared to discuss. When people ask about these accomplishments your body language will be positive, your energy level will rise, your eyes will light up and the story will flow easily! This is another useful method for putting your best foot forward.

References

As you go through the interview process, employers will probably ask for personal references before they're ready to give you an offer. Your goal is to have six references to pick from, but you'll need a minimum of three: two professional references and one personal reference. It's best to identify these people now so you are prepared when asked rather than calling people last minute and putting them on the spot. When the time comes, you can select the ones that will support your candidacy the most.

When you contact a potential reference, ask if they're willing to be a reference, find out what they'd say to a prospective employer, and confirm their preferred contact information. If they agree to be a reference, send them a handwritten thank you note, a copy of your resume and reference document. It's important that you keep these allies informed during your job search, so be sure to update them on your progress.

One of the best ways to create your reference document is to copy the contact information section from your resume. This method guarantees that both documents provide the same professional image and work together. When preparing your reference document, a key objective is to influence what the potential employer and reference will talk about. The best way of doing this is to describe your relationship with the reference and what the reference can tell the employer about you. Review **Job Search Tool 11: References** (p157) for an example. By providing this information, you will guide the reference on key points to share and influence the potential employer on what to ask about.

When an employer requests references, ask specifically how many they would like and the mix between professional and personal. Modify your reference document to include only the number of references requested. Additional references will only slow the process.

Before you provide a reference to a prospective employer, contact the reference so you can brief them on the company and potential position, answer any questions they might have and ensure they're prepared and anticipating the call.

Follow up with each reference to check to see if they were contacted and if so, what the content of the conversation included.

Interview Questions

The final step as you prepare to go to market is to gear up for typical interview questions. Utilize **Job Search Tool 12: Interview Questions** (p158) and **Job Search Tool 13: Behavioral Questions** (p159) for examples of typical questions. This will prepare you to anticipate most questions that pop up while networking, and practice for your interviews.

There are two common traps that job seekers often succumb to when preparing for interviews. First, most people neglect to prepare answers to interview questions in advance. Don't just imagine potential questions and concoct an answer in your head; write out the answers before you go to market! Second, many job seekers don't actually deliver their answers until they're in an interview. You should practice your delivery early and often. Don't wait to practice until just before an interview to "keep it fresh"; that isn't preparation, that's a last resort. Memorization and retention come from repetition, repetition, repetition.

Here's my recommendation. Take the time to write an answer to each potential question and bolster each answer with specific examples from your accomplishments and experiences. Writing out your answers will increase your retention because it's a three-step process:

1. Think about the answer
2. Write the answer
3. See the answer and record it in your mind

Then visualize yourself hearing each question, and respond with your well-thought answer and corresponding accomplishment. Self-visualization is IMPERATIVE! Consider yourself an actor, and each of your lines responding to another actor's question. Go through multiple repetitions, committing your words to memory and speaking them aloud until they're second nature. Pay attention to your body language and see yourself confident and prepared, ready to meet any challenge! You'll be able to answer questions quickly and accurately, which will show your contact that you are well prepared and truly value the meeting.

Be prepared to sell yourself to each and every person you meet. You never know who your next hiring manager will be, so do your prep work now! This is your opportunity to stand out and separate yourself from the crowd—seize it!

PEOPLE HIRE PEOPLE
-Not Resumes

Step 3: Constructing Your Networking Plan

Your Networking Plan will provide focus on your search, educate the people you meet about the networking process and enable your contacts to understand how to best assist you. Use **Job Search Tool 14: Networking Plan Checklist** (p160) to track your completion of the items in this section. As in the last two chapters, you need to continue tracking the time you're investing in your job search using **Job Search Tool 2: Productivity Tracking Form** (p146).

A Networking Plan is NOT a resume. A resume asks: Do you know of a job that I may be qualified for?

This approach puts the person you're meeting with on the spot; turns the meeting into an interview; and if the answer is no, the meeting and conversation will come to a quick end. The contact won't be comfortable providing referrals, as they don't want their colleagues to experience the same discomfort.

A Networking Plan supplements your resume, as it asks different questions:

Is there anyone on my Target List that you can introduce me to?

Do you know anyone that works for any of the companies on my Target List?

Every person we meet knows people we do not. The question is whether they're willing to identify someone they think you should meet and provide that introduction. Since they've already invested time in meeting with you in person, you have a much higher chance that the answer will be yes. By presenting them with a Target List, you make the process *easier for them*.

Are there other people not on my list that I should meet?

Are there other companies not on my list that I should learn about?

This is a great opportunity to learn about new people and companies that you're currently unaware of. This expands your networking options beyond the Target List you created.

By concentrating your actions and words on networking rather than open positions, you clearly communicate that the meeting isn't an interview. This will put your contact at ease and build confidence that you'll approach and treat their referrals in the same professional manner.

Your Networking Plan:

✓   Drives the networking process to generate ongoing referrals.
✓   Educates others about the networking process and how they can best assist you.

✓ Provides focus on the people and companies that are important to you, while opening the door for new ideas.

✓ Demonstrates your investment in the process and shows that you're organized and serious about the effort.

✓ Respects your contact's time by providing organization for the meeting.

✓ Provides enough background information to understand your skills and accomplishments as well as establish your legitimacy as a professional.

✓ Makes it easier for the person you're meeting with.

This is a living document; you should continue to evolve the Target List of people and companies over time. The goal of your Networking Plan is to develop a broad number of contacts within each of your target companies so when that perfect job opens up, the hiring manager will know and contact you before the opening becomes public.

Networking Agenda

The first page of your Networking Plan is your Networking Agenda. The goal of the Networking Agenda is to keep the meeting on-track, productive and short. An agenda demonstrates that you're organized, goal-oriented and respectful of others' time. The biggest benefit you'll gain from your Networking Agenda is that it educates the people you meet on the networking process and how they can assist you.

Your Networking Agenda is a one-page document that contains your contact information and specific topics you want to cover with the person you're meeting. For your heading simply use your name, phone number, and e-mail address. Don't copy your resume header or include your mailing address; the less it resembles a resume, the better. This will focus the meeting on networking, not interviewing. Next, add the topics you'd like to cover during the meeting. A generic agenda works well for 95% of your meetings, but be certain to customize the agenda as you meet with potential hiring managers in Target Companies or specific people on your Target List. Place their name and date at the top of the page and be more specific with the topics and questions.

Networking Target List

Your Networking Target List is a one-page document comprised of three sections:

1. Contact Information – 5% of the page
2. Networking Profile – 25% of the page
3. Target People and Companies – 70% of the page

As with every document you create, include your contact information. Match the format and content used for your Networking Agenda. Your Networking Agenda and Target List should work together so they should look alike.

The Networking Profile section is the 30,000-foot view of your last 7 – 10 years. The objective is to provide the reader an overview of your Transferable Skills, Personal Characteristics, and Accomplishments. As a starting point, copy the Executive Summary or profile from your resume and modify the message to fit the space allowed.

By providing your Networking Profile, you're guiding the conversation in the direction you want. If the contact asks about any of your accomplishments your reaction will be immediate, positive, and natural. You'll have good body language, energy in your voice, and a spark in your eye. Your responses to questions will be powerful and enthusiastic, as you are very close to these topics, and you'll impress the person you're meeting.

The meat of this document is your Target List of people and companies. This section not only should take up the most space but should be formatted so that it's the first thing that catches one's eye. Utilize your list of Target People and Companies from your Marketing Plan to populate your Networking Target List. These two lists must be prioritized into one. The first version should include the companies that best match your background and those you have the highest interest in, as well as the people you want to meet the most. As you network and learn about new companies and people, your list should evolve to stay fresh and expand your focus.

It's critical that for every company listed, you've identified a person that you want to meet. *People Hire People -Not Resumes*, so your primary objective is to meet the people; your secondary objective is to learn about the company. When you have trouble identifying the correct target contact at a company, list the highest person in the organization that you'll feel comfortable meeting. As you gain confidence in your networking skills, you can add the names of people at higher levels in your Target Companies. This doesn't mean you'll meet people on your Target List as soon as you start networking, but it will give those you meet a clear understanding that you're trying to get to a hiring manager.

Part of the networking process is to uncover the correct person to have on the list. When you meet with people on your Target List or those higher in the organization, their referral will get you to others in the organization quicker. It's always better to have introductions flow down an organization, rather than working from the bottom up.

While developing your Networking Target List, pay particular attention to how you organize and arrange your Target Companies. Remember that in Western society, we read top to bottom and left to right, so place the highest priority companies and people on the top left side of the list. This order will create a natural hierarchy, so that if someone starts to read the list and doesn't finish, you ensure that they'll at least see your most important targets.

You should always have more Target People and Companies identified than will fit on your Networking Target List. Create a master spreadsheet document with all of your target people and companies, and continue to add new targets and targets referred by your contacts as your networking progresses. As you meet the target contacts on your Networking Target List, you can remove them from your Target List and replace them with another target. This method allows you to easily manage your Target People and Companies, and also helps you maximize the contacts that you gain while networking.

Keep a Target Company on your list until you've met all potential hiring managers. It's great to have more than one person's name from the same company on your list. The bigger the company the more people you'll need to meet. The more people you know in your Target Companies, the better the chances you'll find out about an opportunity or be remembered when an opening occurs.

When you're referred to someone that's not on your Networking Target List, add their name to the list to use during your networking meeting with them. This will play into their ego and make them feel good, and will help start the meeting on a positive note. If they ask why they're on the list, tell them that you were given their name because they're well connected in the community.

For every person and company on your list, be prepared to explain what the company does, what position the person holds, and why they're on your list. People will ask out of curiosity, and if you can't answer the questions it will hurt your credibility and reduce the likelihood that the person will provide you with additional referrals.

Circle of Contacts

Before you start contacting people, you need a plan of whom you're going to contact and in what order. Calling people at random will waste time and could cause you to miss opportunities. In the previous section, you carefully prepared a Networking Target List, that included names of people you want to network with whether you know them or not. Now add everyone that you know to this list.

You should pull names from:

- ✓ Personal address book - friends, family, spouse's contacts, friends of relatives, and neighbors.
- ✓ Parents from your child's activities - sports teams, Girl/Boy Scouts, Girls/Boys clubs, teachers, coaches, and others.
- ✓ Church directory - people you've met at church or through church organizations.
- ✓ Your child's school directory – families in your child's class.
- ✓ Collection of business cards - vendors, consultants, customers, and functional counterparts in other companies and industries.
- ✓ Past co-workers – include those that left the company before you.
- ✓ Alumni organizations - classmates, fraternity brothers, sorority sisters, and former teachers.
- ✓ Volunteer organizations - members, officers, and board members.
- ✓ Professional and social organizations – members, officers, and board members.
- ✓ Professionals - insurance agents, financial advisors, attorneys, accountants, recruiters, doctors, dentists, and merchants.

Be creative. You don't need to be best friends. As long as you recognize them or they know your name, they should be on your list. The goal here is to have as long of a list as possible to give you the best starting point in your networking. Never assume someone can't be of value in your networking; you may be surprised by who they know.

On your Networking Target List, prioritize each person with the letters "T", "C", "A", or "P" based on the following definitions:

T – Target Contacts - People you don't know personally, but would like to network with. Be aggressive with this list, and never assume someone is out of reach. These people should be included in your Networking Plan as you attempt to expand your network into a new circle — even if they don't work for a target company.

C – Connectors - People you know who work for companies on your Target List or are "connectors." These contacts either have high-level positions in your target companies, or they know lots of other people. These are the people who will move you beyond your own circle of contacts the quickest.

A – Acquaintances - People you recognize from your community, but have had little interaction with. These are people you may have met briefly, but don't know well, though you recognize them by name or face. You aren't sure where they work or what type of connectors they are. These people should be contacted after you have had a few practice meetings, and after your connectors list has been exhausted.

P – Practice Contacts - List of family and friends who you know will say "yes" to meeting with you. When you reach these people, explain that you're calling to practice networking and to obtain their feedback on your performance. These are the safe phone calls.

In the next chapter, you'll develop a phone script to use when placing these calls. It will also be a good opportunity to practice your Transitioning Message explaining why you've begun your job search.

These are your "warm-up" meetings, opportunities to practice before you venture into someone else's circle. They will help build confidence and fine-tune your networking skills before you meet with people on your Target List. These meetings are low-risk; mistakes won't be held against you, but it's CRITICAL that your Practice Contacts watch for mistakes and provide feedback so you can improve in preparation for the real deal. When you meet your Practice Contacts, ask for feedback on your approach and attitude, as well as the overall process. Use your Networking Plan, Agenda and Target List, and make sure the contacts understand what kind of assistance you need from them. Practice your Personal Marketing Story. If you have not settled on one Personal Marketing Story, use one and ask for feedback on your delivery and content. This will help you finalize your message.

These meetings are not just for feedback, but also for referrals. Use your Networking Plan to obtain an introduction to at least one new contact from each practice meeting. However, don't spend the next month meeting with everyone on your Practice List. These are for warm-ups and to build confidence. It's important to get to your Target Contacts and Connectors lists as fast as possible, and get in the game quickly.

When you start making calls, keep the story of the lion and the field mouse in mind. A lion can use his formidable hunting skills to capture a field mouse with relative ease, but no matter how many field mice he catches, he will still be hungry. On the other hand, the lion can hunt for antelope, which are swift and elusive. Hunting for antelope takes hard work and persistence, but the catch is filling and satisfying. Despite the risk and work involved, it is worth the lion's effort to hunt the antelope. If you're only connecting with field mice, it's time to start hunting for antelope—connecting with people who can make a difference in your life. These are the people you have prioritized and categorized as Targets and Connectors.

Setting and Tracking Objectives

The first thing we did in the Preparing for Your Job Search chapter was to establish an objective for how many hours per week you'd invest in your search. Now that you've completed your Marketing and Networking Plans, we need to set objectives for the key activities that will drive your successful job search.

By tracking and measuring your key activities in the networking process, you'll be able to determine if you're investing time in the right areas to get results. Too much time on the Internet can be counter-productive. By tracking how much time you spend on the Internet we can provide feedback on your productivity. If you aren't achieving your objective of meetings per week, we can see if you're making enough phone calls to fill your pipeline of meetings. If you aren't meeting people on your Target List, we can see if you're calling the wrong people, people on your Practice or Acquaintance lists, rather than people on your Target and Connectors lists.

The networking metrics that need objectives are:

1. The number of **hours** you'll invest in your search each week.
2. The number of **phone calls** you'll make each week.
3. The number of **face-to-face meetings** you'll have each week.
4. The number of **hiring managers** you'll meet each week.
5. The maximum number of **hours** on the Internet each week.

You may want to add your own objectives, but these are the core measures for a successful job search.

Each of these metrics measures process rather than outcome. You have control over the hours you work, phone calls you make, and time you spend on the Internet; you don't have control over when you will land. Track activity that measures how well you're managing the process and you'll gain feedback on how productive your search is.

Searching the Web

The Internet is a great resource for researching companies and people. You should always look at a company's website and Google each person before you meet with them. You'll usually gain valuable information about your contact or their company, and have relevant topics to discuss.

However, the Internet can also be a great distraction in your search because there is so much information available.   In the last section, we established the maximum number of hours you'd spend on the Internet. Track and stay true to this objective. Time on the Internet should be for breaks between networking meetings, making phone calls, writing letters, or researching to prepare for an interview.

Searching job boards and applying for jobs online is not the most effective job search method. You can waste hours searching job boards that seem important but won't deliver results. If you insist on using job boards, set up automatic notices so that when relevant jobs are posted, you're notified automatically. Don't just rely on big boards such as Monster or CareerBuilder; identify company, function specific, and local boards in your particular discipline and geography.

If you apply online for a job, follow the directions completely. The simplest mistake, even not copying the correct title into the subject line, could result in your resume being rejected electronically. Avoid applying to blind ads, as it may be your current employer, contingent recruiters collecting resumes, or potentially someone trying to steal your identity.

When you see a position you like and the company is identified, make a direct contact. Build a relationship with an actual person and bring them into your network. Over 70% of all jobs are found via networking, so spend your time effectively for better, quicker results.

Working with Recruiters

Recruiters work for the employer, not the candidate. Their job is not to place you, but merely to fill a position. Don't expect them to give you much time or follow up unless they think there is a potential match. Don't take it personally; they have their own objectives for maximizing their time and getting compensated. Respect their time and be professional. Stay in control of the process by following up with them to obtain updates rather than waiting for them to call.

There are three types of recruiters: agencies, contingent, and retained:

Agencies charge fees to individuals and attempt to place them in open positions. These are typically lower level positions and often they're only available on a contract or temporary basis.

Contingent recruiters are paid by employers to fill open positions. They usually aren't the only recruiter trying to fill the position; they only get paid if they actually find a candidate that is hired.

Retained recruiters are paid by the employer to conduct a search to fill a specific opening. They will be the only recruiter authorized to present candidates for consideration. If you contact the company directly they will refer you to the recruiter for screening.

When you start your search, identify and contact recruiters locally and nationally.   You can identify and research recruiters by looking in the Directory of Executive Search Consultants or Kennedy Red Book. Both are available in the reference section of the library. Find recruiters with expertise in your industry and level of job you are seeking. Specialized recruiters will have many industry contacts and access to hiring manager that can potentially assist in your search.

Meet, write, and talk with key recruiters in order to build a relationship. Dress like each meeting is an interview and bring copies of your resume (and portfolio, if applicable). Use your Personal Marketing Story to let them know what type of position you're looking for.

Never give anyone, especially contingent recruiters, permission to present your resume to a company without your approval. Be upfront with your request verbally, confirm it by e-mail, and keep a copy of their acknowledgement. You don't want your resume going to a potential employer before you make contact, nor do you want multiple recruiters presenting your resume. Debates over placement fees could disqualify you from consideration.

When working with recruiters, follow these general guidelines:

✓ Never pay a recruiter
✓ Never sign an agreement with a recruiter
✓ Always ask if they are contingent or retained
✓ Realize they aren't very effective for industry or career changes
✓ Treat every interaction as if it's a job interview
✓ Don't tell a recruiter anything you don't want the

employer to know
- ✓ Make it clear that they don't have the authority to present your resume without your approval
- ✓ It's okay to give a recruiter the range of your salary requirements

Getting Organized

Continue using whatever method you've used in the past to maintain a calendar. Just make sure that the method is mobile, whether it's a paper calendar or PDA device. If you use a PC-based system, get into the habit of printing out the current and future months so that you always have them on hand. Then you can schedule meetings on the spot rather than having to turn on your PC or wait until you return to your office to check your availability.

Job Search Tool 15: Daily Activity Planner (p161) will act as your daily to-do list and reminder system. A Daily Activity Planner can also help you collect information to assess your productivity and measure how you are performing compared to your objectives. Utilize a Daily Activity Planner each day to guide your job search, record accomplishments, and track your progress.

Many clients prefer to use Outlook or other electronic methods to manage tasks and follow-ups. Staying in control and managing your time is what is critical.

It's extremely important to organize the information that you'll be collecting on people and companies. Once you accelerate your networking and job search, you'll meet too many people and collect too much information to rely solely on your memory.   Set up a procedure to organize and manage this information now, and it will pay big dividends in the future.

Two successful methods I have seen are binders and file folders. If you use binders, create one for people and one for companies. Each tab in the binder denotes a specific person or company. This will allow you to store all the information you have on one person or company in a single place, and you don't have to worry about your computer crashing and losing your data.

If you choose to use file folders, create a file folder for each target person and company. Staple your contact's business card to the inside of the folder and save copies of letters, e-mails, and research completed in their folder. File these in alphabetical order so that you can quickly find any person or company. Use **Job Search Tool 16: Contact Tracking Log** (p162) to record when contact has been made and keep notes on your conversations so you always know the history of your relationship with each contact. As you network, it will be harder and harder to remember all the people you've met, so rely on this tool for memory.

Having contact information when you need it is critical. You need to be able to access contact names, phone numbers, e-mail addresses, your connections to them, and the last time you connected. I suggest using a PDA or a similar device. Each time you meet someone, enter their information into your PDA. In custom field one, enter the name of the person who introduced you to them; in custom field two, enter the last date you connected with them; and in custom field three, enter additional information such as the name of their assistant. This way you can always trace through your network back to your Circle of Contacts and know how you were introduced and the last time you had contact with this person.

I've provided my suggestions on how you can best organize your information, but in the end, the methods are your choice. But no matter how you do it, make sure you're organized from the beginning. Start off on the right foot and you'll have a shorter, more productive job search.

Once the entire Networking Plan section is complete, reward your hard work! You're now ready to start connecting with people.

PEOPLE HIRE PEOPLE
-Not Resumes

Step 4: Connecting with People

Your Connection Plan provides guidelines for the primary methods you'll use to contact people during your search: phone calls and letters. Continue tracking how many hours per day you are investing in your search using **Job Search Tool 2: Productivity Tracking Chart** (p146).

Before you start making phone calls, you need to lay the groundwork for success. Plan what you're going to say ahead of time, and place all your materials at your fingertips.

Phone Scripts
You've picked up the phone, dialed the number, and it starts to ring. What are you going to say when the contact picks up the phone? What will you say when the gatekeeper – the assistant who answers and screens calls for the contact – picks up the phone? What will you say when you reach the contact's voice mail? Now is not the time to carelessly throw together an introduction. You should have your messages prepared before you ever pick up the phone.

Writing out what you will say when someone answers the phone will make it easier to call, and help you present yourself professionally and credibly. It will also make you more efficient, so you can make more calls. Remember that the objective of each phone call is to set up meetings with individuals, not to talk on the phone. Don't become a telemarketer.

Telemarketer Story

Imagine you're at home this evening and you've just sat down for dinner when the phone rings. Reluctantly you answer and a telemarketer launches directly into her sales pitch about a product you have absolutely no interest in. How long will you be on the phone? When I ask this question during my workshops, I get answers ranging from "I hang up" to "Maybe one minute." The most frequent response is "Less than one minute."

Now imagine again that you're home this evening having dinner and the doorbell rings. You open the door and standing there is the same telemarketer selling the same product. How long will you be at the door? When I ask this question during my workshops, I get answers ranging from "A couple of minutes" to "Till she completes her sales pitch." The most frequent answer is "At least three minutes."

The sales person on the phone gets less than a minute of your time, while the same sales person at your door gets at least three times as much time. Why does this happen?

The reason is that when the sales person is on the phone, she isn't a real person. She's just a voice. It's easy for us to hang up, cut off, or be very blunt with a voice. When you open the door and connect a face with the voice, the sales person becomes a real person.

Human nature will give a real person the opportunity to sell, rather than just hang up on the voice.

This is why it's so important during your job search to meet people face-to-face, and not just talk to them on the phone. By meeting with each contact, you become a real person and increase your odds of getting good quality referrals and ultimately the job you are searching for. The phone call is simply a medium to help you achieve your objective – a face-to-face meeting – so that you can sell your product, YOU. Become a real person, and give yourself at least three times the opportunity to sell yourself.

Prepare to make your calls by composing separate scripts for the five situations you're likely to encounter:

1. Calling and getting voice mail
2. Calling and the gatekeeper answers the phone (contact available)
3. Calling and getting a gatekeeper (contact not available)
4. Calling and the contact answers the phone
5. Calling after sending a letter

Review **Job Search Tool 17: Phone Script** (p163) for one example to get you started.

Office Organization
Just as you must be mentally prepared before you call, you must also be physically organized to ensure efficient, successful phone calls. Have the following out on your desk for easy access before you call:

- **Daily Activity Planner** showing who is on your Call List today
- **Prioritized Call List** so you don't run out of people to call
- **Phone Call Scripts** to make the calls easier
- **Transitioning Message** (until it's memorized)
- **Personal Marketing Story** (until it's memorized)
- **Calendar** so that you can immediately confirm availability for a meeting and record the date, time, and location
- **Clock** to time the length of your conversations (less than 10 minutes)
- **Contact Tracking Log** to take notes during the conversation, collect additional contact information (e-mail address, direct dial number, and cell phone number), and to have your referral information available.
- **E-mail opened** so you can send a confirmation e-mail immediately after the contact agrees to a meeting. Confirm the date, time, and location for the meeting.

Networking Phone Calls

To succeed in your phone calls, review and follow these guidelines. They'll help you maximize each call and secure your face-to-face meeting!

1. If you aren't mentally prepared to call, don't call.

You need to sound fresh and energetic while you're on the phone. People can sense a negative tone in your voice, which can lead to a poor impression and kill your opportunity to secure a meeting. If you sense you are not mentally prepared take a 15-minute break and take a walk, call a friend, or read the paper. Get your head straight and then get back to calling.

2. Stay focused on your objective.

The objective of every call is to meet the contact in person, not talk on the phone. Be a real person, not a telemarketer; minimize the time you spend on the phone and maximize the time you spend meeting face-to-face.

3. Respect others' time.

When you reach a contact, always ask, "Is this a good time to talk?" If the person has visitors in their office or is on the way to a meeting, they'll appreciate the consideration. If it isn't a good time, ask, "When is a good time to call back?" Get a specific day and time. If that's not possible, get a day and a general time to call— morning or afternoon. After noticing your consideration of their time on the phone, they will assume you will be just as considerate during a face-to-face meeting.

When you're able to speak with them, limit your call to no more than 10 minutes. If you spend too much time on the phone, the contact will learn too much about you and might not see the benefit of meeting with you in person. Use your phone scripts to start each call to let people know why you are calling: *to network, not to ask for a job*. Your preparation will show you are focused and results-oriented.

4. Treat gatekeepers as well as the contact.

Gatekeepers can have a significant impact on your success. Ask and refer to them by their first names, and write their names on your Contact Tracking Log. Ask them to call you by your first name. Start building a relationship at the first encounter. Enter the gatekeepers' name, direct phone number, and e-mail address into your PDA or whatever tool you use to track contact information.

When you talk with them – either on the phone or in the office – ask questions about themselves, the company, and the contact. Seek their advice regarding other people in the company you should be meeting. View them as an inside connection to the contact and company—they have a great deal of knowledge that can be beneficial to you. If they're willing to refer you to others in the company, it's almost as good as a referral from the contact.

If a gatekeeper has either helped arrange a meeting with a contact or met you at the time of the meeting, send them a thank-you note afterward; treat them as the valuable people they are and reap the rewards!

5. Take great notes.

Record the following on your Contact Tracking Log for each phone call:

- Date and time you spoke with the contact
- What you talked about

- What you agreed to do
- Any required follow-up actions
- When you will call again (enter this follow up in your Daily Activity Planner)

Use your Contact Tracking Log to record your notes, and keep this in the contact's file for future reference. Don't rely on your memory; you have more pressing things to focus on than remembering every single conversation. Once you start meeting lots of people, you won't be able to remember every encounter— what's more confusing, they'll get blurred together! Great notes give you a perfect place to start the next conversation...right where you left off in the last one!

6. STAY IN CONTROL OF THE PROCESS.

You must be the person to call, set up the meeting and follow-up by sending a confirmation e-mail. You'll want to do this for three reasons:

- Make the process as easy as possible for the people you're meeting. The easier it is, the higher the probability that they'll meet with you and assist in your job search.

- Guarantee that there will be a follow-up call. If someone is leaving town and says they'll call when they return, ask when they will return and volunteer to call a day or so later. If you leave it up to them, you can't be sure they'll remember to call when they come back. By taking responsibility for the follow-up call (and entering it in your Daily Activity Planner) you know the call will be made.

- Take the guesswork out of scheduling your next call. If a contact says they'll call, and you don't hear from them that week, when do you follow up? Uncertainty puts you in a bad position. Call too early and you're a nuisance; call too late and you aren't interested. The only way to know the call will happen when planned is to stay in control and handle it yourself!

7. **It's okay to leave a message**.

If the contact doesn't answer their phone, leave a voice message. A message will get you on their radar screen and create name recognition. Your message should include three pieces of information:

- **The name of the person who referred you**
- **Your name and phone number** (if they want to call you back)
- **State that you'll call back and look forward to meeting with them** (from the first contact, emphasize that you want to meet with them— not just talk on the phone)

When leaving a voice message, always spell your last name. Repeat your name and phone number *three times*— once in your first sentence and twice in your closing. Talk slowly and clearly so the person doesn't need to replay the message a second time.

8. Don't send a resume.

Resume requests are a typical delay tactic. By agreeing to send your resume before you have a meeting set, you delay the process by leading with your resume. The relationship starts off as an interview, and provides the contact a reason not to meet with you: "I'm not aware of any openings that fit your background, but if I hear of one I'll keep you in mind."

If someone asks for a resume, push back gently, agreeing to provide your resume for them to review before you meet. Ask again for a specific date, time, and location for your meeting. This transitions the conversation away from your resume and back to meeting face-to-face. However, if someone INSISTS on a resume, then you must send it. Stay in control, though, and agree upon a day and time to call back to set up a face-to-face meeting.

If you're going to send a resume electronically, send it as a PDF. This method ensures that the formatting will be consistent from one version of software to another, or even after passing through different e-mail servers. If you can't save your document as a PDF then send it in Rich Text Format (RTF) rather than as a Word document.

9. Always use first names.

People like to hear their names and are impressed when you remember them. Write their names down in your Contact Tracking Log and enter them in your PDA so you don't have to rely on your memory. Your goal is to develop a personal relationship with this person as a peer, building the relationship with your first contact.

Using first names with a friendly tone will make people more receptive. When you use this approach, many gatekeepers will assume that you have a potentially closer relationship with the contact than you really have, which opens the door to the contact. Use this to your advantage.

10. **Be persistent**.

There is a fine line between being persistent and becoming a nuisance. "Persistence" is calling until you talk to the contact. "Nuisance" is calling more frequently than every third business day.

If it takes 10 calls to talk with someone for the first time, make 10 calls. If it takes 20 calls to follow up with someone, make 20 calls. Don't give up on a contact until they tell you to go away. Second and third calls can be very productive, because the contact has had time to think and can provide additional referrals and information.

Napoleon Hill, in his book "*Think and Grow Rich!*", studied 500 successful people. All shared one trait: **persistence**.

Networking Letters
A phone call is always the preferred option, but when it's not an option, write! Write letters to people on your

target list and community leaders. Letters can act as an introduction and open many doors. Use a letter rather than a phone call when you're uncomfortable calling the contact directly or if the person referring you asks you to write. Send your letters on high quality paper so they'll stand out and get noticed.

The way you approach a person in writing is very similar to calling but more formal. Create your own letter head and use a standard business format. The letter should contain four basic sections.

Paragraph #1 – Connect with the contact and explain why you're writing.

If your referral asked you to write rather than call, lead with this information. The referral reference can open the door and explain why you didn't call.

"I recently met with Renee Referral and she suggested that I write to you."

If your relationship with the person who referred you is a benefit, include the information.

"I recently met with Renee Referral, a fellow volunteer at the YMCA, and she suggested that I write to you."

Always be factual about your relationship with the referral. Never say "my good friend" when you've only met the person once. If you don't have a referral to lead with, the introduction needs to explain why you're writing. This will demonstrate that you've done research on the contact. Attempt to build a bridge between the two of you with a common interest such as a charity or experience.

"Over the last few years I've watched your company grow in revenue, profit, and market share. I'm seeking advice from high performance leaders such as yourself as I consider my job search options."

"We both share a commitment to the Big Brothers Big Sisters organization, but unfortunately we've yet to meet. I'm currently in a job search and am seeking advice from community leaders that share my convictions."

"I've admired your successful career through the years and would like to obtain your advice on my job search."

Be direct and specific to demonstrate that you don't have a hidden agenda.

"I'm requesting twenty minutes of your time to gain your advice on my job search."

"I'm requesting thirty minutes of your time to obtain your advice on people I should be meeting and industries I should be considering."

Paragraph #2 - Your background information.

Include your Personal Marketing Story or the Executive Summary from your resume. Give the reader just enough information to tease their interest without attaching a resume.

Paragraph #3 – Clarify that you aren't asking for a job interview, just advice.

This will put the person at ease, and increase the probability of meeting and obtaining referrals.

"Please understand I'm not asking for nor expecting a job interview."

"I'm contacting you specifically for advice and information, not an interview."

Paragraph #4 – The closing.

End with the specific actions you will take, be respectful of their time, and reinforce that you want to meet with them in person.

"I appreciate your consideration and will call in the next few days to set up an appointment at your convenience."

"I'll call in the next few days to set up a time that we can meet."

"I understand your time is very valuable, and I assure you that I'll be respectful of the time provided."

"I understand that your position is very demanding, and I'll keep our meeting brief."

"I look forward to meeting with you."

Now create three sample networking letters, one using

your Personal Marketing Story, one using your top three accomplishments, and one using your Executive Summary from your resume. When you need to write to someone, use these templates as a starting point for your letters.

The Truth About Networking

Networking is not hanging out in coffee houses, shaking hands, and trading e-mails. Networking is a life skill of developing relationships with people over extended periods of time. It's a give-and-take enterprise that requires equal efforts on both parties. This is why we call it net*working* rather than net*meeting* or net*calling*. True networking is developing a long-term relationship with individuals that will last well beyond your current job search. It's not only whom you know and who knows you, but also how well you know each other.

Some people tell me they feel that networking is asking for help. *This is a mental barrier that you must break through.* Networking isn't a plea for help. Networking is exchanging ideas, sharing resources, meeting and learning about new people, and building relationships. Networking is a two-way street on which neither side owes the other anything because both sides have gained from the experience. Networking is assisting each other to learn, grow, and be successful.

Imagine that networking is a bank. Let's call it The Bank of Networking. With each investment in a relationship, you're making a deposit in your networking account at The Bank of Networking. When you call someone to set up a networking meeting during a job search, you will be making a withdrawal. Your goal is to invest these withdrawals effectively and pay them back with dividends.

As you network, you may connect with people who are unfamiliar with the concept of networking. Explain the purpose of networking to them, and then demonstrate its value by sharing relevant articles, recommending books and websites, passing along job leads, or introducing them to new people. Here's a great way to start the process: ask the person you're meeting if there is anything you can do for them. Start making deposits right away, and as you make additional deposits with people, your relationship will become more and more valuable.

Six-Touch Rule

Each new contact should be "touched" at least six times to start a relationship.

- First Touch: the phone call to set up a meeting.
- Second Touch: meeting face-to-face.
- Third Touch: the follow up e-mail that summarizes the meeting, referrals, and follow-up.
- Fourth Touch: the thank you note you send after the meeting.
- Fifth Touch: follow-up phone call after meeting with their referrals.
- Sixth Touch: invitation to join your network on LinkedIn or Plaxo.

Start Calling

You're now ready to start making phone calls. The way you approach each contact is the same way they'll assume you will approach any referrals they might provide. Whenever you call a referral, you're representing the contact that gave you their name. Be professional, efficient, organized, and express your appreciation with each contact.

When I provide a referral, I give a little bit of my personal reputation away. They will be meeting you out of respect for me, not just interest in you. If you do a good job I get that piece of my reputation back; if you do a great job I get it back with dividends; but if you do a bad job that piece of my reputation is lost forever. Your goal is to make sure that your referral's reputation is enhanced by your actions and words.

Warm up with a few phone calls to your Practice Contacts. Move quickly to your Acquaintances to meet with people you know but are unsure about. Within two weeks, as your confidence builds, start contacting people off your Connectors list. You can start slow, but the faster you meet with Connectors, the faster you will get to your Target People and Companies and the faster you will land.

Your initial calls and the first call each day are the hardest to make, so set yourself up for success. Call a close friend to check on your voice and attitude, call a Practice Contact, call to confirm a meeting scheduled later in the week, or follow up with someone you've already met.

There are no best times to call, so just call. Calling is more important than finding the best time. If you're trying to avoid gatekeepers, call before 7:30 A.M. or after 5:30 P.M. Mornings between 10:30 – 11:30 A.M.

or afternoons between 3:30 – 4:30 P.M. are good times between meetings.

If you leave a message, call back on a different day and time. When speaking with a gatekeeper, ask them for their advice: When is the best time to call? Can we set up an appointment for a call?

Call and meet with as many people as you can. The more people that know you're in a job search, the faster you'll land.

Now that you have meetings set up, it's time to execute those meetings. We will cover networking meetings in Step 5: Executing Your Networking Meetings.

PEOPLE HIRE PEOPLE
-Not Resumes

Step 5: Executing Your Networking Meetings

In the book "*The Tipping Point*", their research concluded that 56% of job seekers found jobs via networking, 19% from ads/recruiters, and 10% by applying directly to companies. This is why we network--to find the hidden job market that doesn't show up on the Internet or in the classifieds. *People Hire People, Not Resumes,* and networking is the vehicle to find the hidden job market, become a real person and land the job you deserve. You're now armed with a Transitioning Message, Personal Marketing Story, resume, and Networking Plan. It's time to set up your networking meetings.

Where Should We Meet?

Your phone call is successful and the contact wants to know where and when you should meet. Focus on making the meeting convenient for them. During the day, try to meet at the contact's office. It doesn't require any travel on their part, costs nothing, and provides you with an opportunity to meet others in their office. Meeting in someone's office almost always results in longer meetings.

You don't want the person to drive out of their way, as this will reduce the time allocated to meeting with you. The best places to meet before or after work are coffee, bagel or pastry shops, and breakfast spots. Each of these locations provides convenience for the contact, are inexpensive, and don't require a big investment of time.

Avoid lunch--it requires too much of a time commitment for the contact, which makes it harder to get a yes answer, and it can be expensive. During lunch there's also too much out of your control such as the service, food quality, and the surroundings. The contact can get too focused on the situation and not on you.

Meeting at a local bar and grill on the way home can be a good alternative to a coffee shop. Let the contact suggest this location; you can never be sure how someone will view meeting at a bar. If you do meet in a location that serves alcohol, order soda or iced tea. This is a business meeting, not a social occasion. After you've made a number of deposits in your networking account for this person and the relationship has been cultivated, then you can enjoy an adult beverage together.

How Should I Dress?

This is a networking meeting, but dress for success! If you're meeting at their office, gentlemen should wear a coat and tie, and ladies should wear a business suit or dress. If the meeting is in a retail store then business casual is acceptable. When in doubt, over dress.

During my search I had a meeting with the Chairman of a large public accounting firm. Their website noted that they had gone business casual year round, and stated that the dress policy was even followed by senior management. I dressed business casual for the meeting, but when I arrived at the firm everyone was in business-wear. As the receptionist led me to the conference room where we were meeting, I saw four people dressed in coat and tie walk into the next conference room. A few minutes later my contact walked in wearing--a coat and tie! The website had overstated the application of business casual, and I felt out of place and my anxiety increased as I realized I had dressed incorrectly. The meeting went great but I never forgot that lesson.

I learned to never rely on company websites for dress code advice. Many companies boast about being business casual, but the unwritten rule is that it only applies to entry-level employees. Don't rely on advice from other employees; your only concern is how your contact dresses, not what the company policy is or how others dress. This is a good question to ask the gatekeeper. Never dress below business casual, regardless of the company, business, or location.

Call to Confirm

Two days before your meeting call the contact to confirm. This is another opportunity to "touch" the contact and demonstrate organization. Confirm the date, time, and location to avoid any miscommunications. It also ensures that you do not waste time by showing up for a meeting that your contact has forgotten about. It took two no-shows for one of my clients to learn this lesson. The first time his contact was called out of town at the last minute. He drove 40 minutes to find this out. The second time his contact double booked meetings. Another 40 minute drive with nothing to show for it. When he finally had the meetings they were very successful but he wasted two hours by not making two, two minute phone calls.

When Should I Arrive?

Arrive 15 minutes early to give yourself leeway for unforeseen delays such as traffic or parking. If you're meeting at their office, you'll have an opportunity to talk with assistants and receptionists. Ask them questions about the company, the contact, and their own careers. If you're meeting with someone from accounting but trying to get to the sales person, ask the assistant/receptionist about the sales person:

"Do you know the Sales Manager Tom Dwaine?"
"Is his office in this building?"
"Do you know his assistant's name?"
"Would you happen to have his phone number?"

All they can say is no.

If you arrive early, the contact will likely start the meeting early, and you can gain more time with them. If you're meeting outside the office, arrive early to secure a place for the two of you to sit and talk. You don't want to waste your meeting time waiting for a table, or end up holding your meeting standing by the door.

If you arrive more than 15 minutes early, wait in the car. Review your Transitioning Message, Personal Marketing Story, and Networking Plan.

Always know exactly where you're going. Use MapQuest or test-drive the route beforehand. If you're going to their office, ask the contact or assistant for directions.

If you're meeting at a retail location, call the store and ask for directions. It's better to ask now, rather than on the way to the meeting. Confirm addresses with the contact to make sure that they haven't moved or are in a different office from the published address.

Once I arrived at a networking meeting well in advance, only to find out that the company had moved. I had looked up the address in a business directory that had been printed nine months earlier but didn't confirm the address with the contact. Luckily, a quick phone call determined that they were two floors up in the same building. If they had moved out of the building I would have been a no-show to the meeting, and my contact may have become a detractor, rather than an ally.

Who Pays?

You're asking for the meeting, so you need to pay. This is another reason to avoid lunch, and get an inexpensive coffee and a bagel instead. Many people you meet will insist on paying, but make sure you offer first. Be appreciative of their gesture, accepting with sincerity. If they pay, make an inexpensive order, like a small coffee and no food.

Networking Meeting Objectives

You have four objectives for every meeting:

1. Get a business card – it provides a wealth of information:
   a. Correct spelling of their name
   b. Direct dial phone number
   c. Correct mailing address for your thank you note

    d. Correct title of their position
    e. E-mail address
    f. Mobile phone number

2. Learn something that will aid your search:
    a. New people to put on your target list
    b. New companies to put on your target list
    c. Industries that are doing well
    d. Successful transitioning experiences
    e. Different approaches in your networking
    f. Their career path
    g. Feedback on your approach and presentation

3. Referrals to keep your networking alive:
    a. One from your target list or someone that works for a company on your target list
    b. One from a company not on your target list, but their recommendation
    c. Someone else in their company (for large organizations)

4. Make deposits in your Networking Bank account:
    a. Offer assistance to each person you meet
    b. Make suggestions to solve a problem
    c. Recommend books, articles, or websites
    d. Provide introductions to other people

How Long Should We Meet?

Networking meetings can last from 10 minutes to as much as an hour. The contact will determine how much time they're willing to invest. It's your responsibility to keep track of the time; live up to the request you made and give the contact the opportunity to close the meeting on time. If the meeting is productive, many

people will offer additional time. Have a mental plan
on how much time you will spend on each agenda
item based on the total time you've agreed on. See
the following suggested timetable for a 20-minute
meeting.

Agenda item	Minutes
Introduction, Thanks, and Business Card Exchange	2
Transitioning Messsage and Personal Marketing Story	2
Advice on Search and/or Career History	4
Networking Contacts	10
Follow-Up, Offer of Assistance and Thanks	2

What Should I Do During the Meeting?
You asked for the meeting, so regardless of the location
you should act as the host and initiate the dialogue.
This is your time to take the lead and talk.

Make direct eye contact with your contact and welcome
them with an introduction, firm handshake, and thanks
for taking the time to meet with you. It's important to
show your guest that you're glad to see them and that
you view him or her as an important person.

*"Hi Steve, I'm Frank Danzo. It's good to meet you!
Thank you for taking the time to meet with me today."*

If you're meeting at their office, follow their lead to the

location of the meeting. Don't take a seat until they do or they offer you one. You don't want to sit in the seat they had planned for themselves or at the wrong end of a table. If they offer a beverage and you want one, accept it with appreciation.

If you meet at a retail location, greet them at the door, show them to the table you've saved, and offer to buy a beverage.

"Hi Steve, I'm Frank Danzo. Thanks for meeting with me today. I saved seats for us over here. Let me buy you a cup of coffee."

Wherever you meet people, use heartfelt candor rather than witty remarks. You never know how others will react to jokes or comments. Be and share yourself, and you'll build a relationship and make deposits in the Bank of Networking. Smile and enjoy yourself. If you think and act as if the process is painful, so will the person you're meeting with.

Offer your business card and if they don't offer their own card, ask for it. This will ensure success with the first objective of a networking meeting.

"Steve, here's my business card. Do you have a card with you?"

After you've spent time getting to know the contact as a person, provide them with copies of your Networking Plan (Agenda and Target List). Remember, the person and relationship comes first and networking second. Have copies of your resume available but only provide it if asked. Even if you sent your resume in advance, don't assume that they read it or brought copies with them. Always bring extra copies of each document. The contact may spill something on the document, write on it and want a clean copy, or introduce you to someone that you can share your extra documents with.

As you hand out the documents, explain the purpose of each one. People like to hear their name, so use it often and it will help you remember them and they will remember you.

"Steve, I prepared an agenda for our meeting. I find that an agenda helps me stay on task and makes meetings productive. I'd like to share some background information on myself, obtain your advice, and review a list of my target people and companies to see if you can introduce me to any of them."

It's critical that you educate your contact on the networking process and set the expectation that you would like them to introduce you to someone else.

"Let's take a look at my Networking Target List, which is the second page I handed you."

Share your Transition Message to get it out of the way. It's better to get it over with and move on rather than have them ask later in the meeting.

"During a recent reorganization my position with American Chemical was eliminated."

Share your Personal Marketing Story and reference the accomplishments outlined in your Networking Target List.

"Steve, I'm a marketing professional with experience in marketing strategy and determining lines of business development. My strengths include marketplace and competitive analysis, qualitative and quantitative research methodology, and product design. I've succeeded by leading and teaching others and by being a team player that works well with cross-functional teams. By identifying opportunities for product expansions into new markets, we grew our market share by 10%. An organization based on integrity and needing market share growth would benefit from my marketing expertise."

If the contact asks questions, keep your answers concise and focused on the last seven years. If they ask about one of your accomplishments, share the Accomplishment Story you prepared for your Marketing Plan. Stories provide a flow and are easy to remember and pass along to others.

For a 20-minute meeting, this should take no more than four minutes. You want to provide a snapshot of your background and experience, but too much information will make the meeting feel like an interview. Review **Job Search Tool 18: Networking Meetings Time Allocation** (p164) for suggested time allocation for a 20 and 30-minute meeting.

Throughout the meeting, NEVER ask or talk directly about a job! This topic will put the contact on the spot and make them defensive. It will most likely shorten the meeting and decrease the likelihood of getting any referrals. Have faith in the process and your contact's intelligence; if they're aware of an opportunity, they'll bring it to your attention. If they do suggest an opportunity, show interest by taking detailed notes on the information provided and follow up. When you get to the point of asking for referrals within their organization, this is a soft way of asking about job opportunities within the organization.

Now it's time for your contact to talk. Ask for advice on your search or about their career.

"Steve, what would you do if you were in my shoes?"

"How have you made changes during your career?"

Always take notes and consider advice you receive during your networking, but only implement advice that you agree with. Everyone has an opinion but that doesn't mean that their opinion is right for you. This is your search, so stay in control and take full responsibility for every step of the process.

Once you obtain their advice you need to move on to your target list of people and companies. Lead the transition with open-ended questions such as; "Do you know any of the people on my Target List?" You always run the risk that the contact won't engage the way you'd like. In these cases you need to be prepared to ask additional follow up questions. Review **Job Search Tool 19: Networking Meeting Transition Questions** (p165).

As the contact responds to your questions, good listening skills are very important. Humans think 500 – 600 words per minute, but we talk 100 – 200 words per minute. Review **Job Search Tool 20: Good Listening Skills** (p166). Listening isn't easy, so stay focused and keep these skills in mind.

For a 20-minute meeting, this should take no more than four minutes. During this time you'll need to balance receiving good advice, being polite, and looking for an opportunity to transition to your target list. When you have the opportunity, transition the conversation from advice to your target list. This is where you want to spend the majority of your time.

"Thanks for the advice, Steve, attending the Professional Marketing Association meeting next week is a great suggestion! I'll look at their website to get the details on the meeting. Steve, based on my research my Networking Target List has a list of people that I'm trying to meet and their companies. Is there anyone on my list that you could introduce me to?"

Give them time to look through the list and answer the question. Patience and silence work to your advantage. Remember this is the time for the contact to think and talk, so don't fill the silence with comments and other questions. Let your contact absorb and process the information on your Networking Target List. If they offer a referral, write down the name and ask for contact information, preferably a phone number. Read the contact information back to them to make sure you've written it down correctly. Specifically ask if you can use their name as a reference when you call.

Since you want to stay in control, don't ask your contact to call the referral. If they offer to call, politely thank them but state that you want to make this easy for them so you don't mind calling. Offer to call first, and if you don't reach the referral, tell your contact that you'll contact them for assistance.

"Steve, I appreciate your willingness to call on my behalf but I don't want to burden you. Let me call first, using your name as a reference. If I'm not successful, I'll contact you for assistance."

If your contact insists on contacting the referral, you must follow their lead. In this case, clarify when you should follow up with them. You'll avoid calling too early and being a nuisance, or too late and not showing interest.

"Steve, I appreciate that you'll call to provide an introduction. When should I follow up with you if I haven't heard anything?"

If the contact doesn't know anyone on your target list, look for a stepping stone, someone that works for a target company but isn't on your list.

"If you don't know the specific person on my target list, is there someone else that works for any of these companies, whom you could introduce me to?"

Again, patience and silence work to your advantage. Let them think and respond.

The next step in the process is to expand your target

list based on their knowledge.

"Steve, based on what you've learned about me and my situation, are there other people you know that you'd be willing to introduce me to? Are there other companies that should be on my target list? I don't want to restrict myself just to my target list."

Be patient. Give your contact time to think and process your questions. If they work for a large company, the last step is to ask about referrals in the company. This is a soft way of asking about opportunities within the company.

"Steve, is there anyone else in your organization that you think I should meet?"

For a 20-minute meeting, your goal is to spend 10 minutes securing new contacts. It's your responsibility to keep track of the time. When the end of the meeting approaches, attempt to close the meeting.

"Steve, it's almost 8:00 and I promised not to take more than 20 minutes of your time."

This will demonstrate respect for their time. If your contact wants to continue, they will take the lead.

"Steve, I enjoyed meeting you today and I appreciate the referrals you provided. I'll be approaching them the same way I approached you for advice and referrals. I'll summarize my notes and email them to you."

Summarizing your notes and sending them to your

contact makes it easier for them. It's a way to get their e-mail address if it isn't on their business card; makes another impression in their memory; and allows you to again say thank you. Sometimes a second connection can be very productive because it gives you another opportunity to prompt them for additional referrals. I've had contacts that didn't provide any referrals during the meeting, but did during a follow up e-mail. I always thought that they were testing me to see if I would follow-up.

As you succeed at obtaining referrals, you're making a withdrawal from your Networking Bank. To make a deposit, always offer assistance to your contact.

"Steve, is there any way that I can assist you today?"

Since you're building a lasting relationship, find out the best way to stay in contact.

"I'd like to stay in contact with you so I can update you on my success with your contacts and let you know where I land. Do you have a preference on how to reach you?"

"How often would you like an update, monthly?"

Then round out the meeting by thanking the contact one last time.

"Thanks again Steve! Have a great day."

Every person can teach you something, so don't rush to a conclusion that you're wasting your time.

Sometimes the last three minutes of a meeting are the most beneficial. If you show disinterest, your contact may shut off and you won't receive any referrals.

Saying Thank You

After you've met with a contact, send them a thank you note. It should be handwritten, brief, and addressed personally, not with a title like "Ms." or "Mr.", but by first and last name. A handwritten note will stand out from e-mails and form letters. Express your sincere gratitude and thank them for their time and referrals. Refer to something that you talked about during the meeting to make the note personal and unique. Remind the contact of any planned follow up, and then close with another thank you for their time and assistance.

Dear Steve,
Thank you very much for meeting with me today. I appreciate your suggestion to attend the Professional Marketing Association meeting, the referrals provided and the words of encouragement. I'll update you on my success with your referrals after I meet with them.

Thanks again and I'll stay in touch.

Frank Danzo

Write the note in the office lobby and drop it off with the receptionist. Your contact will receive the note while you're fresh in their mind, and you'll avoid the possibility that the note gets lost in the mail. Furthermore, the details of your meeting will be easy to recall, and you'll have another opportunity to make an impression with the receptionist or gatekeeper.

Likewise, be sure to write the gatekeeper a thank you note! Use their first name and thank them for facilitating the meeting and the information they provided. Make a deposit in the Networking Bank, and build the relationship so they'll open the door whenever you call.

Dear Pam,
Thank you for setting up my meeting with Steve. It was great to meet you and I appreciate the advice you provided. The meeting wouldn't have been a success without your assistance.

I will keep you updated on my progress and let you know where I land.

Thanks again,

Frank Danzo

Once you've sent the initial thank you note, conduct future contact by e-mail or phone, whichever is their personal preference.

Networking Events

Networking events aren't social events – they're part of your job search. Treat them just as you would an individual meeting. Research the opportunities and make a target list of events you'd like to attend. Not all events are equal in value, so focus your efforts and invest your time wisely. As with a networking meeting, practice your Transitioning Message and Personal

Marketing Story before you arrive. Be on time and dressed for success! If alcohol is served, minimize consumption by drinking soda or alternating between alcohol and water.

Plan Before Attending Networking Events

What type of people will be there? Is this a community event or professional organization?   Research the event and seek advice from others that have attended in the past to gauge the value of attending. Is there anyone in particular that you're trying to meet? Is there a particular company you want to make a contact in? How long do you plan on staying?

If you dislike these events, make them a challenge and game. Set objectives:

"I'm free to leave after meeting three, five, or seven new people."

"I can leave once I get three good contacts to agree to meet in the future."

Research the industry or organization to have something current to share with others. Have two to three current events that you can bring up to start a conversation. Focus on local business news, and avoid politics and religion. Succeed at filling your networking pipeline with future meetings, and reward your efforts by leaving!

When you go with a friend, it's too easy and safe to talk with them and not meet anyone new. If your friend is a member that can introduce you to others, then take advantage of the introductions. If you feel

uncomfortable going alone, then include your frie⎤
your planning and agree on your objectives. It's best if both of you drive, so if you or your friend decides to leave the other can stay. If you drive together, agree ahead of time how long you will stay, what type of people you can introduce each other to, and have a signal that you would like to leave. After an introduction from a friend, agree that your friend should excuse themselves so that you can talk with the person one-on-one.

When you call to register for a meeting, volunteer to work the reception table. This is a great way to feel included and the perfect opportunity to meet attendees by introducing yourself to everyone that comes to the table. During this time you can plan on whom you'd like to talk to after the reception table closes. Since you've already met them at the reception table, don't be shy about introducing yourself again and striking up a conversation.

What to Bring to a Networking Event
- ✓ **The currency of networking events is business cards, so bring lots of your cards!** Trade business cards with everyone you meet. Exchange business cards so you can call them the next day to set up a networking meeting.
- ✓ Two pens and a small note pad to take notes. Write when and where you meet each contact, who introduced you, and what you talked about on the back of their business card. This information is a great starting point for your follow up call.
- ✓ A PDA to check your calendar if someone wants to set up a meeting on the spot.

After the networking event, e-mail each person you met within 24 hours. Send a short message letting them know you enjoyed meeting and talking with them; confirm that you're interested in meeting and you'll call in the next couple days to set up a convenient date and time.

For each person you e-mail, call them within three business days and ask if you can meet to learn more about them and their business. Look for opportunities to make a deposit in the Networking Bank and demonstrate your value as a networker. If you believe that you've made a great connection, don't wait; call them the next day! If you wait too long they may not remember or think it wasn't important to you.

You're now ready to hold efficient and effective networking meetings. Get started so you can generate interviews and land successfully. Good luck, you'll do great!

PEOPLE HIRE PEOPLE
-Not Resumes

Step 6: Acing the Interview

If a job candidate's skills and experiences match the job requirements, why wouldn't they get an offer? In most cases, an offer wasn't extended because the candidate committed one of many common interviewing mistakes. Before we discuss the proper steps you should take to pass your interview, I'd like to point out some potential landmines.

- Not preparing thoroughly
- Dressing down
- Not demonstrating why you're the best choice
- Not selling yourself enough (being too modest)
- Dominating the conversation
- Talking very little and appearing disinterested
- Mentioning compensation too early
- Focusing on compensation
- Badmouthing past employers and bosses
- Failing to ask questions
- Lack of enthusiasm about the position
- Poor personal grooming
- Negative attitude
- Failing to follow up after the interview

Now that you're aware of these mistakes, you can avoid them and prepare for success!

Generating Interviews

In my experience there are five general methods of generating an interview, listed in order of highest success rate.

1. Networking
    Networking creates more than five times the interviews as any of the other four methods. This is why you've spent so much time and effort preparing and directing your energy toward networking. At the same time, you can't ignore the other four sources of interviews. Use these methods efficiently and focus your time on the method that gets results— networking!

2. Applying directly to a company
    For companies that are on your target list, review their websites weekly. Many websites will allow you to register a profile and select keywords that relate to your job. When those keywords show up in a job description or title, you will get notified with an e-mail, which is more efficient than looking at multiple websites each week. Be sure to check the websites of your target companies on the weekend; find these postings as early as possible and take action before others do! Utilize your networking to identify and contact the hiring manager directly.

3. Recruiters
    You may have identified specific recruiters in your Personal Marketing Plan and contacted them as part of your initial networking. Once you get on their radar, send them a status update each month. Investing additional time and energy with them is

unproductive. If they have a potential job match, they'll contact you.

4. Job boards
Searching job boards can feel productive, but it's the least efficient method of the five as it can consume lots of time. In Step 5, you established a goal of the maximum hours to spend on the Internet; continue to track and stick to your goal.

Many job boards have overlapping postings, so don't spend time on every website. Identify a limited number of job boards you will monitor, including specialty boards for your expertise or geography. Register a profile and sign up for e-mail notifications so that you don't waste time on the Internet instead of networking. Enter as many keywords and titles as the system will allow, providing the widest coverage possible. If the system won't accept the number of keywords or titles you want to use, set up a second profile by either using or deleting a middle initial. Use the technology to your advantage so you can spend your time meeting people.

5. Print ads
Print ads are the least likely source of job leads so limit your time in this area. Each week you should review publications which can provide potential job opportunities. Focus on specific publications in your industry and expertise or the largest local paper and business journal, not every paper and trade magazine that exists. Look for companies that have recently won new business, expanded their office space, or hired new employees.

Cover Letters

When you've identified an open position, customize your cover letter and resume to the specific job. Include key words from the job description in both documents. This increases the odds that your resume will be selected if it's initially screened by a computer.

Utilize the marketing tools you developed in your Personal Marketing Plan, such as your Top Transferable Skills and Personal Characteristics, to construct a powerful cover letter. The letter should be no more than one page and consist of three paragraphs.

Paragraph #1 - Specify the position you're applying for, note the source and date you saw the opportunity, express positive interest in the position and state that your skills and experience match the requirements. If you're responding to an online posting, there is no need to reference the website or date.

Paragraph #2 – Present your qualifications. There are many ways to present your skills and abilities. These are three of my favorites:

1. Share your Personal Marketing Story.
2. Use bullets to connect the key job requirements with your accomplishments.
3. Use a Requirements versus Competency Comparison (RCC) Chart-style paragraph (discussed later in this chapter).

No matter which format you choose, select the optimum words from your Top Transferable Skills and Personal Characteristics lists to demonstrate expertise in each job requirement and describe yourself.

Paragraph #3 - The closing paragraph should again express positive interest in the position, request an interview and state when you will follow up. The search is yours, so keep control of the process by following up on your application, rather than waiting and hoping for a response. If you don't have a specific person to follow up with, state that you look forward to exploring this opportunity further in person.

If the company is identified in the ad or posting, drop off a copy of your cover letter and resume to the company as well as mailing, e-mailing and applying online. Having your cover letter and resume considered electronically, by mail, and in person increases your odds of a response. When providing a hard copy of your resume, print it on high-quality paper, not copy paper. Address the cover letter to the attention of the hiring manager. If you don't know who the hiring manager is, address it as directed in the ad or posting. Call the company and ask for the manager of the department you would be working in. Your goal is a face-to-face meeting, so be persistent and direct.

Customize a cover letter for every open position. You needn't make dramatic changes from one cover letter to the next; just adjust your Top Transferable Skills, Personal Characteristics, and accomplishment examples so that they address the job description as best as possible. Before you send a cover letter, have your coach and a good friend proof the document. Misspelled words or poor grammar will definitely disqualify you from consideration.

Invited to an Interview

You have successfully networked your way to uncovering a great job opportunity. The hiring manager has asked you to participate in an interview. What do you do now? Understand that interviewing is a process, an exchange of information between you, the candidate, and the people conducting the interview to answer eight key questions.

Will you?

Employers' Perspective	Candidates' Perspective
Can you do the job?	Do I want to do the job?
Do you fit in our culture?	Would I fit in their culture?
Can you work with our employees?	Can I work with the people I have met?
Can we afford you?	Can I afford to work here?

Unless the answer to all eight questions is yes, an offer shouldn't be extended or accepted. Not every job you interview for will be a good match. It's better to find out now that you won't be happy or successful, rather than after you start a job.

The biggest mistake you can make when you get an interview is to stop networking. You have no assurance of getting the job or that you even want it; that's what the interview process will determine. If you don't get the job and haven't continued networking, you'll have a void in your schedule and it will feel like you're starting over. This is a great time to network as your confidence is high and you have specific job opportunities to talk about.

Participate in all interviews, especially early in your search, even if you know you don't want the job. You may find out that the job is very different than you understood and be more interested than you first thought. Even if this position is not a good match, the company may have other openings that they'll consider you for now or in the future. The more interviews you participate in, the clearer you'll understand what you're looking for and the better you will perform in networking meetings and future interviews. Use these as practice which will prepare you to perform your best when you interview for the job you really want.

The goal of the interview process is to get an offer. The objective of each step in the interview process is to get to the next step, not to get an offer. Getting too far ahead of the process can send mixed signals and could disqualify you for the wrong reason. That's why it's important to find out how many steps are in the interview process either before you begin interviewing or during the initial interview.

When you're first contacted for an interview, ask the following questions:
⊙ How many candidates are participating?
⊙ How many rounds of interviews will there be?
⊙ Is any formal testing required?
⊙ What's the time line for completing the process?

The better that you understand the overall process, the

better you'll be prepared and perform.

Setting an Interview Appointment

When you're called to set up the date and time for an interview, try to avoid first thing in the morning or the end of the day. You want to avoid potential traffic problems getting to an interview or finding out that the hiring manager isn't a morning person. Likewise, at the end of the day people may be tired, disgruntled from a bad day, or in a hurry to leave. If the employer already has a schedule, follow their lead and make the best of the situation.

During the call, ask for these details:

✓ A job description (if you don't have one)
✓ The name(s) of the person or people that will be interviewing you
✓ The correct spelling of their name(s)
✓ Their job title(s)
✓ Their relationship to the hiring manager
✓ How long they've been with the company
✓ How long they've been in their current position
✓ Whether it will be a private or panel interview
✓ How long each interview will last
✓ The location of each interview
✓ If you need to arrive early to complete any paperwork
✓ If you should bring anything or be prepared to cover any specific subjects

Research Before the Interview

Now that you have the interview scheduled, it's time to complete your research on the company and people you'll be meeting. Start by visiting the company website. If they have a search function, search on the department you'd work in, the product or service you'd be supporting, and the people you'll be meeting. If they don't have a search function, use the "Find" feature on your web browser to do the same thing. Read any news releases from the last 12 months to be familiar with current events, new product introductions, key financial or sales results, or promotions.

Google the company, product or service, and the people you'll meet. This is a good way of learning an outside perspective of the company and its people. Search the archives of the Wall Street Journal, local business journal, and newspapers for any recent articles on the company or people.

Your research should provide an understanding of the financial health of the company, their position in the industry or how they compare to the leader, current events for the company or industry, what opportunities or threats are present for the company or industry, and their reputation in the community as an employer.

Rely on your network to learn more about the company and people you're going to meet. Send individual e-mails out to specific people in your network telling them you have an interview, including the name of the company, title of the position and a list of the people you'll be meeting. This is a great way of reconnecting with your network and updating them on your progress. Ask your network if anyone can provide information on the company, their products or the people you'll be meeting. You never know who knows whom or who can provide valuable information.

If the public can access the company's facility, visit just like a normal consumer to see what the facilities are like and how they treat people. If you can purchase the company's products, try them out. If you know someone that has used their product or service, ask them what they liked and disliked. Contact one of their vendors and ask how they are to work with.

After completing your research, you'll be better prepared to develop relevant conversation starters, demonstrate your knowledge of the company, match your unique skills and experiences to the job requirements, and formulate probing questions to ask during the interview.

Preparing for the Interview

In most situations you'll have 30 – 60 minutes with each person to sell yourself and convince them that you're the best candidate. Be active in this process, and show up armed with information and a plan.

There are five documents to bring to your interview:

1. Requirements vs. Competency Comparison (RCC) Chart
2. Questions to ask each person
3. Integration Plan for the hiring manager
4. Closing Statement
5. Agenda

With any interview, you must establish credibility that you have the skills and experiences necessary to do the job. A one-page RCC Chart will help you guide and focus the dialogue in the direction most beneficial to you. Your goal is to prepare a document that will demonstrate through accomplishments that you have the skills and experiences necessary to be successful in the position.

This is an expanded version of the RCC paragraph used in your cover letter format. Utilize a two-column table with the left column titled "(Job Title) Requirements" and the right column titled "(Your Name)'s Qualifications". In the left column, summarize the job requirements based on the job description, website posting or conversations before the interview. Use the same words and phrases that the company uses so that it's easy for the interviewers to quickly recognize the description. In the right column, list specific accomplishments that demonstrate success with each requirement. This will help guide the dialogue and questions toward the accomplishments which you've already prepared as Accomplishment Stories in your Marketing Plan. Use your list of Top Transferable Skills and Personal Characteristics to select the proper words to describe your expertise in each job requirement.

If you don't have experience directly related to a job requirement, do not include that specific job requirement. You don't want to highlight any shortcomings in your skills and experiences. If asked why you didn't list all the requirements, reply that this is a summary of key requirements and you wanted to limit the document to one page. Review **Job Search Tool 21: RCC Chart** (p167) for an example.

As part of the interviewing process, you'll want to

obtain information to assist in making your decision. Prepare a list of questions that you want to ask about the company, products or services, and the position. Have specific questions for each person and more general questions that you'd like to ask to multiple people. Asking the same question to more than one person can provide great insight on an organization. Prioritize your list so if the time is limited, you can ask the most important questions first. Be careful not to put anyone on the spot by asking them to provide feedback on your candidacy. Avoid questions about salary or benefits; it's best to let the employer initiate dialogue on compensation. The employer has more cards in their hand, so let them play them first.

For the hiring manager, prepare an Integration Plan demonstrating what you would accomplish during the first 30 – 60 – 90 days after you start. This should be a one-page document outlining key objectives and actions that you would suggest. Title the document "Draft" so that the hiring manager knows that you're looking for his or her input and guidance to complete the plan. The intent of the document is to show the hiring manager that you're goal-oriented, demonstrate initiative, and communicate your preparation for the interview. Pay close attention to the key job requirements from the job description to make sure you're focused on fulfilling these requirements. Address key challenges that your research has uncovered, understanding customer needs, develop relationships with peers and employees, and hold planned feedback sessions with your hiring manager to ensure you're on track.

Next, prepare a Closing Statement for the interview.

When an interviewer prepares to close the interview by asking, "Is there anything else you would like to share with me?" or "Is there anything else you would like to ask?" have your Closing Statement ready. Thank each person for the opportunity to interview for the opening, highlight your critical Transferable Skills and Personal Characteristics, note an accomplishment that demonstrates your expertise in the most significant job requirement and enthusiastically communicate that you want the job. Write out your Closing Statement and practice. You want to be perceived as confident, prepared, and enthusiastic. This is the time to strut your stuff and win the job!

The final step is preparing the agenda, a one-page document that will guide and focus the dialogue with an interviewer. The objective of this document is to make sure you share the information you feel does the best job of selling yourself, while obtaining information so you can decide if you're interested in the position. Before you leave the interview you should share and obtain enough information to answer the eight questions every interview should answer. Your agenda will help you achieve this.

Treat the open position, not you, as the subject of your meeting. Based on the questions you've developed, list the topics that you want to cover during the interview(s). You can utilize one agenda or customize the agenda for each person; just make sure you cover the information needed to answer the eight interview questions! The agenda can be used as a checklist for yourself or can be shared with each interviewer to help guide the dialogue. How you use the agenda, to share it or not, is based on your comfort level with the people you're meeting. If you aren't comfortable sharing the agenda, you should still prepare it, bring it with you, and use it as your checklist to ensure a productive interview.

What to Bring to the Interview

The excitement of an interview can cause you to forget simple but necessary items such as business cards, references, breath mints, or money. Consult **Job Search Tool 22: Interview Checklist** (p168) the day before an interview, gather the items, then do a final check on the day of the interview.

Dressing for an Interview

When in doubt, over dress. Business dress is always recommended and will allow you to look your most professional. If the hiring manager or HR manager recommends business casual for your interview, then dress accordingly, but you should NEVER dress less formal than business casual!

Business Dress
    Men – A pressed suit, shirt and tie
    Women – A conservative dress or business suit

Business Casual
    Men – A collared shirt, slacks and a jacket
    Women – A blouse, slacks and a jacket, skirt and
        blouse, or dress

Casual (**NEVER**)
    Never dress casually, even if given the option

Make sure your shoes are polished and in good

STEP 6: ACING THE INTERVIEW   115

condition.   Be conservative with make-up, jewelry, perfume, or cologne. For these items, less is best. Personal grooming is also critical to making a great first impression. Be freshly bathed, clean-shaven, with a recent haircut and manicured fingernails.   Before you go to an interview, get a second opinion on your clothing and accessories from your career coach or Support Chain.

Practice, Practice, Practice

Just as professional athletes fine-tune themselves with a warm up or practice before competing, business professionals must also hone their skills prior to competing for and winning an interview. Each of your networking meetings is a mini interview where you'll gain experience and confidence.

In preparation for your interview, review the following documents and practice:

- Transitioning Message
- Personal Marketing Story
- Accomplishment Statements
- Accomplishment Stories
- Resume
- Portfolio
- Interview and behavioral questions and answers
- Research on the people and company
- Requirements versus Competency Comparison (RCC) Chart
- Questions to ask each person you'll meet
- Integration Plan
- Closing Statement

Review and study the documents, then ask your career coach and Support Chain to conduct practice interviews and provide feedback. The more you practice, the more comfortable you'll be and the better you'll perform during the real interview.

The Interview

Confirm the location and directions for the interview. Use MapQuest to verify the directions and estimated travel time. Plan on arriving 15 minutes early. If you arrive more than 20 minutes early, park and review your documents before you go in. Before leaving your car turn off your mobile phone, pager, etc. You don't want any distractions during the interview.

When you go to an interview, view it as a stage production. All eyes will be on you to see how you "act". You'll be judged by the way you dress, walk, stand, sit, shake hands, give eye contact and deliver your "lines". This is why you need to prepare both physically and mentally to be onstage. The way you present yourself will make a difference in the hiring manager's mind!

Introduce yourself to the receptionist or assistant, shake their hand, make eye contact, smile, remember their name and tell them who you have an appointment with. It's best if you visit the restroom to check your appearance before introducing yourself. If this isn't possible, introduce yourself and then ask for directions to the restroom. Check to make sure your hair is combed and clothes are neat.

While you're waiting, ask the receptionist or assistant questions. This is a great opportunity to start collecting information to assist in making your decision.

"What do you like most about the company?"

"How long have you worked for the company?"

"What do you like most about working for your boss?"

For each person you meet, follow the same steps. Be the first to introduce yourself, shake their hand, make eye contact, smile, and use and remember their first names. People need to believe that you're glad to be there. Look for the opportunity to provide a compliment, or use a "fun fact" from your research to jumpstart the conversation.

"What a great picture of your family!"

"How long have you been involved in the American Cancer Society?"

Be engaged in the process and with everyone you meet. Don't underestimate the influence of anyone, regardless of their position. In my experience as a hiring manager I always asked my assistant what she thought of potential candidates. If my assistant didn't approve of a candidate, they would be rejected.

Stick to the agenda and subject at hand. Don't ramble or go off on tangents. Listen carefully to each question and provide an answer. If you don't understand the question, paraphrase to check your understanding or ask for clarification. Interviewers will sometime ask inappropriate or borderline illegal questions about your age, religion, health, or marital status. Once a question is asked you must respond, and how you respond is important. Many times it's a case of an inexperienced interviewer. Try to understand the issue driving the question, rephrase the question to verify your understanding, and answer your rephrased question. Not answering the question or challenging the interviewer might make you feel better, but will not help you advance to the next step in the process.

References

Before the interview, notify your references that you have an interview, confirm that you can provide their name, and thank them for their support. Provide the company and/or person's name that will contact them so they can anticipate the call. Share your research so they know what the company does and the title and general responsibilities of the position. Provide suggestions on the key points that you'll be making in the interview so they can support your efforts. This will prepare them for the call if it's made.

Ask them to contact you if they are called so that you can get their feedback on the questions asked, any comments made and the general feel of the call. To stay in control, let them know you will call after the interview to provide an update. Remember to thank them for their time and support.

Thank You Notes

After the interview, send a thank you note to each person that interviewed you. Thank them for their time and the opportunity to interview for the position. Check your notes from the interview and refer to something that the two of you discussed to make the note unique to them. Express interest in the position, provide an example of why you feel you're the best candidate, and state that you look forward to working with them in the future. Close with another thank you for the opportunity to be considered. If you're writing to the hiring manager, include a timetable for you to follow up. Make sure the notes are not carbon copies of each other, as some companies collect thank you notes and compare to see if they are duplicates.

Don't forget to write the gatekeeper or assistant a thank you note. Thank them for facilitating the interviews and providing information or advice. Build your relationship with them so when you call back to follow up, the assistant will help you connect with the hiring manager, rather than being a barrier.

Write the notes in the lobby or car before you leave. This will ensure that they get written timely while the information is fresh in your mind. Drop the notes off at the receptionist's desk rather than in the mail. This way the notes will show up in the interviewer's mail the same or next day while you are fresh in their mind and avoid the cost of postage.

Negotiating an Offer

Those that speak first usually lose. Avoid talking salary as long as possible. Let the employer bring up the topic of money. The employer has more cards in their hand so let them play their cards first.

When asked, be honest and accurate on your salary history. You may be asked to verify your last salary with a copy of a check stub or W-2. This is especially true if you're in sales and a significant portion of your compensation was commission.

When given an offer, don't accept on the spot. Acknowledge the offer:

"Thank you for giving me the offer."
"When do you expect a decision?"
"I'd like to discuss the offer with my family."
"I'd like to review the benefits package."
"I want to make sure all my questions are answered."

This gives you time to consider the offer, create other offers, and ask questions you've formulated since the interview.

Once you've received the offer, contact any other companies that you've been talking with about potential openings. Only contact companies that have a position that you're interested in and would seriously consider taking.   Let them know you've received an offer and the time frame that you need to respond to the company. Don't bluff. You aren't using this as a negotiating chip with your existing offer; you're doing this to create another offer so you have more options. Having more than one offer can push you to make an objective decision.

Compare the job and offer to what you wanted and what you wanted to avoid in a job from your Personal Marketing Plan. This will help you be objective about your decision.

Almost anything is negotiable. The higher the position or smaller the company, the more open the negotiations. **Job Search Tool 23: Negotiation List** (p169-170) is a list of potential items to negotiate.

Any negotiation should be a win-win. Compare your offer to the job requirements from your Personal Marketing Plan and determine what is important. You need to justify why you're asking for more than was offered and outline the benefit to the company. Agree on salary and other cash compensation items before you address non-cash benefits. If you're asking for more money, do your homework on market rates so that you can use this data in your request. If they say no, ask if you can have a six-month review to reconsider your request after they have seen the value you are adding to the organization. Ask only about issues that are important, not because it would be nice. Like any negotiation, it's a two-way street. Asking for too much, just because you can, could result in the offer being withdrawn.

If you're leaving a company, be careful about using another offer to get your current employer to give you an increase in pay. This could be a short-term strategy, as your employer will always question your loyalty in the future. When you submit your resignation, be prepared to leave that day. Many companies are terminating employees immediately, rather than giving them continued access to computer systems and company information.

Once you have a verbal agreement ask for it in writing. The offer must be on company stationary, outlining key areas of compensation, especially if they are different from the standard package, including any contingencies they're stipulating such as reference checks. Ask when you can pick up a copy of their benefits summary, new employee packet and other material they'd be willing to share.

If a company or person isn't willing to put an offer in writing, this should send up a red flag. Ask why the offer won't be put in writing. If you're resigning from a company, wait until you receive an offer in writing and all contingencies are released. You don't want to end up resigning from your current job, only to find out that the hiring manager lacked the authority to offer you the new job.

Accepting an Offer

Accept the offer both verbally and in writing. Call the hiring manager to share your decision, express gratitude and excitement for the opportunity, and confirm the start date. Follow up this conversation with a written acceptance letter referencing the offer letter and agreed start date.

Get involved in your new organization quickly. Ask to review and have input in your announcement to the new organization. Update your Integration Plan and send it to your new boss to discuss on your first day. You want to understand your working relationship with your new boss such as frequency of meetings, preferred method of communication, expectations for the first week and month, specific projects that you will be working on, who inside and outside the organization you should meet immediately and a specific timetable to receive feedback during your first 30-60-90 days.

Now that you've landed, your networking shouldn't stop. The next phase in networking is keeping your network alive.

PEOPLE HIRE PEOPLE

-Not Resumes

Step 7: Keeping Your Network Alive

Congratulations, your hard work has paid off! You've accepted an offer and are excited to start the next chapter in your career. Plan a celebration to reward yourself; you deserve it! But before you begin your new job, you need to reconnect with your ENTIRE network and share your good news.

It may sound like a lot of work, but there are two main reasons for reconnecting with everyone. First, your contacts contributed knowledge, introductions, and moral support during your search, and you should let them know that *you made something of their assistance*. It's always good to reaffirm your value and show that others, such as your new employer, believe in you too. People enjoy good news and will be glad to learn of your success.

Secondly, your job news provides a natural opportunity to reach out and refresh these connections. Strengthen your relationship with them, and they'll be more likely to approach you in your new capacity as a business partner, or even contact you about future job opportunities that may interest you.

So get to it! Contact everyone in your network and share the good news. Thank them for their support and offer your assistance in the future. Besides receiving your offer, these will be the best meetings, phone calls, and e-mails that you'll make during your entire job search.

There are a number of best practices that you should hold firm to during this outreach. When you're trying to determine the proper course of action, follow this simple rule: the stronger the relationship or the more assistance a person provided, the more personal the contact should be. For many this means a simple phone call; for others, meeting and sharing a mini celebration. But in most cases, this contact can be by a personalized e-mail.

If you want to engage a contact in direct dialogue but can't meet in person, a phone call is the next best method to show your gratitude, because you're able to clearly express emotion and other verbal cues. If your contact doesn't answer, don't leave a voice mail message and call it quits. Such behavior is inappropriate because:

1) It's impersonal
2) It places the burden of returning the call on the contact, which can lead to a frustrating game of phone tag
3) It can be a one-way communication that isn't returned

Avoid this debacle by leaving a message that you called to share good news, and inform them that you'll call again, placing the burden squarely on your own shoulders.

Now is not the time to cut corners. NEVER send a mass e-mail thanking your contacts, as your recipients may perceive such a generic communication as impersonal and lazy. Draft a message that states where you landed and what you will be doing; then confirm their contact information and thank them for their assistance. Cut and paste the message into individual e-mails, customizing the opening and/or closing paragraphs with information that is relevant to each specific person. In closing, be sure to mention that you'll provide your new contact information once you get started. This gives you a good reason to follow up with them in the future.

Postal mail is a last resort. Compared to the preferred methods of contact, postal mail is time-consuming and expensive, slow to arrive and easily lost in the shuffle. Postal mail should only be used when you don't have a contact's e-mail address, or if you can't reach them by phone. If you must use postal mail, follow up with a phone call to obtain an e-mail address and other contact information for the future. Postal mail is also a means to follow up and provide contacts with your new business card, but in the digital age, an Outlook or LinkedIn vCard (electronic business card) is better than a paper card that can easily be lost.

In addition to the people who assisted you during your search, there is an often-overlooked opportunity afforded by such good news: to contact each company where you interviewed and have yet to receive feedback. Call the hiring manager directly to withdraw your name from consideration. Thank him or her for the opportunity, provide an update on your success and verbalize that you would like to stay in contact with him or her in the future. Convert this person from a hiring manager to part of your network.

As the final step to close out your job search, update your resume so it's current and ready for new accomplishments. You've already learned that you should always be prepared and have control over your own career; make certain that you're in the driver's seat and never let an employer direct your career again.

You've successfully landed, built a great network, closed out your search and are excited about starting your new job. Now you can abandon your network and move on.

ABSOLUTELY NOT!!!!!

Now isn't the time to stop networking; in fact, you should be networking for the rest of your life. Rather, it's time to shift your networking priority from job search to relationship building. Focus on making deposits in The Bank of Networking and increasing the value of your networking account by developing long-term relationships. Whether you ever go through another job search or not, a strong and well-funded network will support your future success.

Networking: A Life Skill

Networking is one of the most important life skills you can ever learn or teach. During your job search, you learned how to network successfully, and if you're like me, you were continually amazed by people's generosity. Of the hundreds of new people I've met the last few years, there are only two that refused to meet with me, and one other that didn't provide referrals when we met. That gives me about a 99.9% success rate of converting phone calls into productive meetings in which I secured new relationships, valuable knowledge, and additional contacts for my network. I think that success rate is incredible, not just because it shows that this system works, but because it highlights the other half of the networking equation: people are *naturally* generous and willing to assist you.

During a meeting with the President of ARCO Construction, Jeff Cook, I asked him why he was so willing to assist me with my job search. He responded, "Some people think life is a race and they need to get to the finish line first. I agree it is a race, but I think we should all get to the finish line together." His answer has inspired me to be a better person, not only in helping others network and find their jobs, but in all aspects of my life.

Make Others Successful First

You have a choice with every person you meet: you can pass the time with empty conversation, or you can share part of yourself and develop a meaningful relationship. There's always a risk of rejection, but the potential for a deeper relationship makes it all worthwhile. Whether in business or your personal life, ultimately it's the people you know and how well you know them that will make the difference.

My wife's grandmother always said that every time you gave a dollar to someone in need, you'd receive two dollars in return. Your dollar didn't need to be real money, nor did what you received in return, but the value would be there. The same is true of networking; it's all about the law of reciprocity.

Reciprocity guarantees your act of kindness will be repaid in the future. Time and time again, you realize more of a return on your investment than the person you helped, because giving not only delivers tangible results, but it feels good too. The more you care about the other person, the more you'll go out of your way to help them be successful. When you care for others, they'll care for you. That's the power of generosity, the true currency of networking.

The best way to become special to someone is to make them feel special. When you reengage with someone, focus on what you can do for them, not what they can do for you. You will develop a broader and more valuable network by being interested in others' successes than trying to get them interested in your own.

Make deposits in The Bank of Networking, and know that the investment will assist someone in their success today. Your payback may not come today or tomorrow. It most likely won't even come from the same person. But have faith; the payback will come.

Growing and Maintaining Your Network
Invisibility is the failure of networking. Never ever disappear. You've invested too much time and effort in developing your network to let it die. The relationship between visibility and networking is like sunlight to a

plant. Without it the plant will wither and die. With it, the plant will grow strong. You've already developed the roots of your network; stay visible and keep yourself open to new and better relationships, and you'll succeed in cultivating new branches for your network.

Your network may seem rather amorphous, but plug all of your contacts into a business connection service like LinkedIn, and suddenly you can see your network as a living, breathing entity. LinkedIn can make it easier to stay connected with your network, and Plaxo can help keep your network's contact information current. But remember, personal contact is always valuable and necessary; an online connection to your contacts' latest information isn't the same as being current in your relationship.

Organizing and Managing Your Relationships

To continue developing your network, assess what type of relationship you have with each person in your network. Understanding your relationships will help you prioritize which relationships require or deserve the most investment. There are four basic relationship categories that we can place people into:

1. Acquaintance "AC" – **Someone you only know slightly.** These are people you met at a social or business event, were introduced to for the first time, or recognize by sight and name, but haven't had any significant interaction with. You know who they are, but nothing more. Very little effort has been invested in this type of relationship, and if left alone for the short-term, the networking account will fall dormant and ultimately close.

2. Associate "AS" – **A professional or social relationship.** You've met these people more than once and have had a reasonable amount of time to get to know them. You know where they work, their profession, and general information about their family and personal life. At the very least, this level of relationship requires a minimum investment of several touches per year.

3. Ally "AL" – **A relationship of mutual support.** This is someone you would feel comfortable calling and asking for a favor, would be happy to do a favor for, and given the opportunity, would do a favor without being asked. This type of relationship requires regular deposits in your networking account with contact by e-mail, phone, and face-to-face meetings.

4. Advocate "AD" – **A relationship where either would intercede on the other's behalf.** This is someone that you subconsciously think about and would go out of your way to assist without being asked. You share a high level of trust. The advocate is the most valuable relationship to have both personally and professionally. Once your networking account grows to a balance this large, the relationship is strong enough to be self-sustaining.

Frequency of contact is NOT the measuring stick for your networking relationships. You could have frequent contact with a good friend because you enjoy their company, but in terms of networking value, they may only be an associate. Rather, networking relationships should be measured by the willingness of each of you to assist the other. Someone that you see infrequently could actually be a much stronger ally or advocate.

Technology can be a valuable tool for managing your network. As you go through your contact list, categorize each relationship into one of these four categories. Use these categories as a sorting field in your PDA, contact software or Excel spreadsheet. Now you can quickly look at your "Ally Network" and see whom you need to "touch" to make a deposit in their networking account.

Keeping Your Network Strong

Your network is like a muscle. The more you work it the stronger it gets. Left alone, your network will become lazy, weak and useless, so repetition is important. Regular contact with people will strengthen your network. Whether via e-mails, phone calls, meetings over coffee, or mailing an interesting article, staying on your network's radar screen is vital. The closer the relationship, the more personal the method of contact should be. Each succeeding touch will strengthen the relationship and increase the value of your networking account. Whether you are selling, buying, looking for a great candidate, or simply looking for advice, a strong network is a great asset.

Look for reasons to contact people such as birthdays, relevant changes in your life or theirs, book or article recommendations, or just check to see how they're doing. Don't wait for the year-end holidays to contact everyone. Many people get flooded with holiday well wishes and your message can get lost in the crowd. Furthermore, never forward chain e-mails to your network as an excuse to stay in touch. Such e-mails will be irritating and in bad taste, and you run the risk of alienating people, so that when you actually send an important e-mail, they won't read it.

Your current relationship and the level of relationship you would like to have will determine the investment required. **Job Search Tool 24: Relationship Guidelines** (p171) provides suggestions for the time you need to invest to strengthen your network. The chart provides advice on the frequency and type of contact to maintain or build your relationship. The left column reflects your current relationship with a contact: acquaintance, associate, ally, or advocate; and the top row reflects the future level of that relationship. The point at which these two meet will feature advice for driving your relationship from where it currently stands to where you want it to be.

As an example, if you consider yourself associates but want to progress to allies, find the associate level in the left column, and then follow that row to the right until you are under the ally column. Your objective is to interact with the contact at least quarterly through a combination of e-mails, phone calls and face-to-face meetings for the next year to build up your deposits in the networking bank.

Lack of contact can also reduce the level of your relationship. If your relationship is at the ally level in the left column, it could deteriorate to the associate level if you don't have contact for more than one year.

Diversity in your network is important. Get to know people from different industries and professions.

Maintain a top ten list of people you would like to meet and share this with your contacts. The best way to expand and strengthen your network is to touch as many different circles as possible, and connect your circle to new circles.

Always encourage the people you meet to stay in contact. An open-ended invitation with no commitment leaves the door open so you can look for ways to help them succeed. Increase the value of your networking accounts, build your relationships, and stay atop people's radar.

To truly be a networker, you need to be viewed as a "connector". People contact you because of who you know and because you always provide assistance. Being able to connect different people and assist in their success is one of the most rewarding things you can do in your life. True networking is grounded in helping others and giving more than receiving.

By exercising, expanding, and sharing your network, you will add a new level of security and satisfaction to your life. Regardless of what challenges you have in life, you will be better prepared to turn these challenges into opportunities and ultimately, successes. Pass along the gift of yourself and the life skill of networking to everyone that you meet.

PEOPLE HIRE PEOPLE

-Not Resume

You Can Do This Too!

There are few things more rewarding than coaching Job Seekers to come alive in the eyes of Employers.

In a resume, all applicants look pretty much alike. When it arrives on a prospective employer's desk, it just lies there, looking uniformly like every other resume.

Most have little or no personality, for resumes are distillations of a person's career into a page or two of factual statements. Merely the facts.

So what's a job seeker to do? What does it take to be noticed, interviewed, and hired? What does it take to come alive?

I've been answering that exact question for thousands of applicants for more than 10 years now. And I assure you, there are few career paths more rewarding – both emotionally and financially -- than helping a job seeker get his or her career back on track.

Looking for a job is a big job in itself -- one that can overwhelm even the most educated, skilled, and experienced applicants. It's not something they've done very often, if ever. Most have had limited experience looking for a job, and they're therefore not very good at it.

Have you ever been in that situation? Have you ever had your confidence shattered when you found yourself in strange waters without the knowledge needed to navigate them? Have you ever lost your job unexpectedly?

I have, and it was not a pleasant experience. But I was very, very lucky to have had a job that prepared me well to speak on the subject and for a stimulating new career as a career coach.

Actually, I began by coaching other business people as an employee of a Fortune 50 company. Fellow employees always seemed to feel comfortable approaching me for help and support. I enjoyed being a "sounding board" and prided myself on giving sage advice.

As my responsibilities grew, I was given the opportunity to create a leadership development course. In the process, I saw how coaching can be an extremely powerful career path. As a coach, I directly influenced the careers of fellow employees and indirectly touched the lives of the people *they* worked with. In some cases, I could even see how the lives of their family members were affected as well.

When it came to an end for me, I was stunned. *Downsized* was supposed to be a word in someone else's vocabulary, never mine. My employer seemed embarrassed when they told me but, "Don't worry," they said , "We will provide you access to an outplacement service to help you."

And I believed them. I didn't worry at first. I assumed that the outplacement company would teach me everything I needed to know to land the job I wanted.

Yet while under the outplacement company's roof, it quickly became clear to me that they were actually a kind of adult daycare center. They provided an office space where fired employees could hang out while applying their very limited search skills and experience to finding a job.

Sure , the service provided a form of job-search training and materials. They were encouraging and very positive in their outlook, at least at the start. Yes, they listened to our problems and gave comforting advice.

But when it comes to showing job seekers exactly how to actually accomplish face-to-face meetings with hiring authorities, outplacement falls short.

Job seekers need to know what to do, when to do it, and most importantly, how to do it. They need to be shown how to develop both a strategy for targeting their employment goal, and the step-by-step tactics to reach it.

The outplacement firm had exposed me to *their* idea of a job search. But they just didn't recognize what business professionals in transition need most.

They need a really special breed of coach. One who

knows a search system that works and how to teach that system to job seekers. Someone who can be understanding one minute and just as demanding the next.

That special coach could very well be you.

Sure, I'd been a coach of other business professionals. But the real test came when I was forced to apply what I knew about networking and job searching to myself. Through trial and error, I determined what worked best.

Even after I landed a great job, I continued to refine my system. When people in my network became displaced, they would call me and ask for contacts or help in getting a job. My answer was always the same: *"I can give you a name and a phone number, or I can show you how to network your way into a better job."*

Of course, I always added the warning that, *"It won't be easy, but if you follow my instruction, it will work. And you'll probably get into a better job situation faster than by any other search method."*

That's not all. I wanted to help, but I wasn't about to waste my time and theirs unless they also clearly understood: *First, effective job searching is hard work, period. Next, my instruction will require you to step out of your comfort zone. Third, you will have to learn new skills. And finally, to keep you on-goal, you will be accountable to me.*

Over the years, thousands have taken me up on my offer

to help. Along the way, many of the men and women I've trained began to use my system to help others get jobs. Then things snowballed. More and more people came to me for training. And an increasing number of my graduates turned to me for help and advice as they were mentoring others.

But before we formalized our system and gave it the name *Career Networking Pro*, we added a 21st century refinement – the internet connection, which effectively places CNP coaches "in the same room with" the job seekers they're helping – regardless where each of them is located!

Picture that in your mind for a minute. Our system works. It has proven itself over and over. Then it grew on its own when people I'd coached passed along that training to others. Until we made it a web-based process, all of us were pretty much confined to working with job seekers, face to face. With the internet, we can still maintain that very important in-person relationship, only online.

As the CNP System matured, we also found that *job seekers are willing to pay a lot of money for a job-search system that generates quality leads and timely results.* Why? Because it's *worth* it. Our system gives them a realistic shot at landing their dream job. And it's a proven way for them to find a great job often *months* faster than they would have on their own.

Yes, CNP is a proven system. But its effectiveness relies heavily on the human element. Some person – some man or woman – must deliver the training and oversee it. That same trainer must be a pesky coach that holds the job seeker accountable for applying all aspects of the system.

That special coach could very well be you.

If you decide to join us, you'll make an initial investment to pay for training, software and support in running your CNP Trainer business. While the business model is extremely organized and structured, you will have many choices as to how you apply it.

You may choose to focus on a broad range of job seekers in your area of the country, or concentrate on the sector/industry you know best. You can also approach HR departments directly, demonstrate how well the CNP system works, and gain the business that had previously gone to outplacement firms!

And here's the icing on the cake: Very few thrills in life can match the excitement and satisfaction you'll feel every time a client calls to say they just received an offer for the position that's at the top of their list. Knowing that you contributed to their success is a pretty amazing feeling. Besides, you'll have made a friend for life!

One final re-reminder – applying the CNP system is not easy. But it's definitely worth it because it works. The same is true for building a successful and rewarding business as a Career Networking Pro Search Advisor. It, too, is worth it because it can work for you.

Of course, I would never expect you to decide to join us strictly on the basis of this book. So please call us today at 877-542-5940 for free information and to start your own due diligence into becoming a Career Networking Pro Search Advisor.

You can make a big difference in the lives of others, and in your own, as a respected CNP Search Advisor. It's worth it because it works.

Best regards,

Frank V. Danzo

Job Search Tool 1

Preparation Plan Checklist

Activity	Date Completed
Productivity Tracking Chart	
Daily Routine Plan	
Office Set-up	
Job Search Coach	
Support Chain	
Motivations and Rewards	
Recommended Readings	
Contact Information	
Business Cards	
Thank You Notes	

Job Search Tool 2

Productivity Tracking Chart

Objective: I will work _____ hours per week

Day of Week	Week Of	Week Of	Week Of	Week Of
Monday				
Tuesday				
Wednesday				
Thursday				
Friday				
Saturday				
Sunday				
Total				
Objective				
Variance				

Job Search Tool 3

Office Checklist

☐ "Office" location _____
☐ Desk or table
☐ Comfortable chair
☐ Adequate lighting
☐ Phone
☐ Voice mail or service
☐ Computer
☐ Printer, scanner, copier, fax combination
☐ Internet access
☐ File cabinet or filing system
☐ File folders – for tracking contact information
☐ Hanging folders for filing individual file folders
☐ Paper/notepad for taking notes
☐ Printer paper
☐ 9" X 12" sized envelopes
☐ High-quality paper for resumes and cover letters
☐ High-quality envelopes
☐ Postage stamps
☐ Stapler
☐ Pens and pencils
☐ Stopwatch/clock for timing phone calls
☐ Three-ring binder for your Daily Activity Plan
☐ Calendar
☐ Contact tracking software
☐ Your personal motivation (see Step 2)
☐ Radio (background music)

Job Search Tool 4

Marketing Plan Checklist

Activity	Date Completed
Productivity Tracking Chart	
Transitioning Message	
Transferable Skills	
Personal Characteristics	
Accomplishment Statements	
Accomplishment Stories	
Personal Marketing Story	
Target People	
Target Companies	
Resume	
References	
Interview Questions	

Job Search Tool 5

Transitioning Message

Reorganization

During a recent reorganization, my position with Specialty Chemicals was eliminated. I look forward to using my sales and marketing skills to drive sales and increase market share in the chemical industry.

Merger

As a result of the merger between Phelps Electronics and Global Communications, 15% of the workforce was eliminated, including my position. I am now exploring opportunities in the electronics industry to take advantage of my engineering and management experiences.

Downsizing

With the recent downturn in the construction industry, Blair Construction reduced its workforce by 10%, including my position. I plan on using my project management skills to assist owners or general contractors to complete projects on time and within budget.

Job Search Tool 6

Transferable Skills

Communications	People	Thinking
Concise	Approachable	Analyzing
Honesty	Coaching	Critical thinking
Persuading others	Flexible	Judgment
Teaching	Leader	Logical
Training	Respectful	Process
Public speaking	Teamwork	Quality

Organizing	Function
Accountable	Accounting
Follow-up	Distribution
Implementing	IT
Planning	Marketing
Restructuring	Project Management
Scheduling	Sales

Job Search Tool 7

Personal Characteristics

Personal Style	Attitude	Interpersonal Style	Work Habits
Assertive	Adaptable	Appreciative	Assured
Calm	Big Thinker	Candid	Autonomous
Committed	Creative	Collaborative	Confident
Dedicated	Flexible	Competitive	Decisive
Determined	Generous	Considerate	Dependable
Driven	Hopeful	Diplomatic	Efficient
Eager	Imaginative	Direct	Firm
Energetic	Inquisitive	Empathetic	Flexible
Excited	Inspired	Engaging	Focused
Honest	Kind	Enthusiastic	Hard Worker
Intelligent	Optimistic	Innovative	Insightful
Intuitive	Original	Level-headed	Leader
Motivated	Passionate	Loyal	Logical
Perceptive	Pioneering	Open	Organized
Predictable	Practical	Perfectionist	Productive
Prudent	Rational	Personable	Quick Thinker
Resourceful	Realistic	Persuasive	Resourceful
Self-Aware	Relentless	Probing	Responsible

Job Search Tool 8

Accomplishment Power Verbs

Achieved	Converted	Fulfilled	Mapped
Activated	Created	Gained	Merged
Added	Cultivated	Generated	Minimized
Advanced	Cut	Headed	Modified
Advertised	Deciphered	Honed	Mounted
Agreed	Decreased	Identified	Negotiated
Amplified	Delivered	Improved	Obtained
Announced	Designed	Included	Opened
Applied	Developed	Increased	Operated
Arranged	Devised	Inducted	Organized
Attained	Diminished	Innovated	Perfected
Augmented	Directed	Inserted	Piloted
Automated	Discovered	Installed	Pinpointed
Began	Distributed	Instigated	Planned
Branded	Drove	Instructed	Printed
Built	Employed	Integrated	Processed
Caused	Enhanced	Intended	Produced
Changed	Enriched	Invented	Promoted
Circulated	Ensured	Invested	Proposed
Clear-cut	Envisioned	Issued	Published
Collaborated	Excellent	Kicked off	Ran
Commenced	Executed	Launched	Realized
Conceived	Extra	Lessened	Reduced

Job Search Tool 9

Personal Marketing Story

I am a Marketing professional who has been successful at identifying new opportunities and leading capture teams to secure long term contracts. My strengths include relationship building with customers, business case analysis, and an ability to network to identify new opportunities. I also have a native fluency in Italian & Spanish and a strong command of German which I have used successfully working with many international customers. My successes have been driven by coordinating team activities to meet customer needs and company goals. I have secured long term contracts valued up to $40 million in the aerospace market. I am eager to transfer these skills to a new industry with significant international interests.

Job Search Tool 10

Resume Guidelines

Overview

- Expect to undergo multiple revisions before creating a final product.
- The first half-page of the resume is the most important; invest the time in this section to give it the most impact.
- Use a short, direct, and active writing style.
- Always be truthful, factual, and accurate.
- Ensure that your contact information, e-mail, and phone number will not change during – and preferably beyond – your search.
- Your most recent experience (the past seven to 10 years) is the most interesting to a potential employer.
- Begin each accomplishment with a power verb.
- Use numbers, percentages, dollar amounts, or other metrics to quantify accomplishments.
- Avoid using "I," "me," or "my" in your statements.
- One version of your resume is enough. Modifying your resume to include key words based on a job description makes sense, but only when a specific job is identified. This is the time to include the correct buzzwords, highlighting accomplishments that match the position requirements.
- If you update your resume during your search, do not go back and send new copies to people you have met.

Job Search Tool 10

Resume Guidelines

<u>Appearance</u>

- Customize the look of your resume so it does not look like you copied a template.
- Limit the resume to two pages. It is acceptable to list only job titles for positions more than 10 years old. This will allow you room to focus on your most current experience.
- Include a heading, as well as your contact information, on the second page.
- Use white space, so your resume is visually attractive, professional, and uncluttered.
- Use wide, even margins to increase the amount of space for information.
- Use 10-point or 11-point Ariel or Times New Roman typeface.
- Write out all numbers up to, and including, nine. Use numbers for 10 and above.
- Use bullets, boldface, and lines to guide the readers' eyes.
- Label each section of the resume clearly.

Job Search Tool 10

Resume Guidelines

<u>Do Not</u>

- Mix responsibilities and accomplishments.
- List references or include the phrase "references are available."
- Include any personal information such as marital status or number of children.
- Include a picture.
- Use abbreviations.
- Overuse capital letters, bolding, and underlining. Use industry jargon that others will not understand.
- Use odd-size paper, colors, style, or fonts. A resume should look like a resume.
- Let a paragraph or bullet run over to the second page. Keep thoughts together.
- Use "K" or "M" abbreviations. Use the actual number for thousands, and spell out millions.

<u>Quality Check</u>

- Make sure the resume supports your Marketing Plan providing a consistent message.
- Make sure the resume works with, and supports, your Personal Marketing Story.
- Ask at least two other people (one person from within your industry, and another with expertise in English or Journalism) to review your resume for clarity, understanding, and mistakes.

Job Search Tool 11

References

TODD J. RUFFTONE, MBA

818-578-4398(cell)   465 Pool Drive
rufftone@e-mail.net   Burbank, CA 91056

References

Mr. Steve Clark
Vice President Š Corporate Human Resources
Large Corporation, Inc.
Glendale, CA
818-357-5948 (office)

Mr. Clark was my direct supervisor from 1995 to 2001. Steve can provide insight on my skills in leading multiple operations, planning and organizing major projects, and developing leaders.

Mr. Tod Fine
Vice President and General Manager
Distributing Company, Inc.
Los Angeles, CA
265-913-6834 (cell)

Mr. Fine was my direct report for over ten years in two locations. Tod can provide feedback on my P/L management, communication, employee development, and planning skills.

Mr. Paul Bristow
Vice President Business Development
Communications, Inc.
West Ridge, CA
818-314-9852 (cell)

Mr. Bristow was a supplier to Large Corporation, Inc. Paul can discuss my strategic planning, communication, organizational, and relationship-building skills.

Mr. Brian Bank
President
Bank of Beverly Hills
Beverly Hills, CA
818-456-7891 (office)

Mr. Bank and I have been friends for over ten years. Our daughters played on the same soccer and basketball teams, and our families attend the same church. Brian can share with you my qualities of teamwork, compassion, patience, and high integrity.

Job Search Tool 12

Interview Questions

1. What aspects of your last work experience relate to this position?
2. What do you consider to be your greatest weakness?
3. Why are you leaving (or did you leave) your most recent position?
4. Why should I hire you?
5. What can you tell me about the strong and weak characteristics of your last boss?
6. What was the toughest work decision you ever had to make?
7. What changes would you make if you came on board?
8. How would you overcome your lack of experience?
9. Have you had experience firing people?
10. How would you describe your leadership style?
11. What examples can you give me of: Your creativity? Analytical skills? Managing ability? Other skills?
12. What is the toughest work challenge you've ever faced?
13. What do you look for when you hire people?
14. What was the toughest part of your last job?
15. How do you define success...and how do you measure up to your own definition?
16. What is the most common misperception about you?

Job Search Tool 13
Behavioral Questions

1. What would be an example of a time when you had to go above and beyond the call of duty in order to get a job done?
2. Sometimes it's easy to get in "over your head." What would be an example of a situation in which you had to request help or assistance on a project or assignment?
3. Can you recall a situation where you worked with a colleague who was not completing his or her share of the work? What did you do? What happened?
4. What kind of situation have you experienced in which you had to arrive at a compromise or guide others to a compromise?
5. In a supervisory or group leader role, have you ever had to discipline or counsel an employee or group member? What was the nature of the discipline? What steps did you take? How did that make you feel? How did you prepare yourself?
6. Can you describe a time when you were not satisfied or pleased with your performance? What did you do about it?
7. Can you describe a situation in which you found that your results were not up to your supervisor's expectations? What happened? What action did you take?
8. Can you describe the most difficult decision you have had to make? How did you make the decision?
9. Have you ever experienced a time when a customer, co-worker, or employee was very upset with your work? If so, what did you say and do?

Job Search Tool 14

Networking Plan Checklist

Activity	Date Completed
Productivity Tracking Chart	
Networking Agenda	
Networking Target List	
Circle of Contacts	
Setting and Tracking Objectives	
Searching the Web	
Working with Recruiters	
Getting Organized	

Job Search Tool 15

Daily Activity Planner

Daily Activity Planner

Today's Date [　　　　]

Meetings

Total Meetings [　　]

Time	Person	Location	Notes	*

* I = Interview   H = Hiring Manager   T = Target List   C = Connectors   O = Other

Phone Calls to Make

Total Phone Calls [0]
S = [　]   M = [　]

#	Name	*	#	Name	*	#	Name	*
1			11			21		
2			12			22		
3			13			23		
4			14			24		
5			15			25		
6			16			26		
7			17			27		
8			18			28		
9			19			29		
10			20			30		

* S = Spoke with Contact   M = Left Message

Letters to Write

Total Letters [0]
N = [　]   J = [　]

#	Name	*	#	Name	*	#	Name	*
1			2			3		

* N = Networking   J = Job Specific

Things to Do

#	Item	*	#	Item	*
1			4		
2			5		
3			6		

Hours Worked Today

Meetings [　]   Phone Calls [　]   Letters [　]

Research [　]   Internet [　]   **Total Hours Worked** [0]

Job Search Tool 16

Contact Tracking Log

Name of Contact		Company		Position	
Phone (Work)		E-Mail			
Phone (Cell)		Phone or E-Mail (Alt)			
Referred by		Relationship with Contact			
Referral Phone		Referral E-Mail			

Date	Notes Taken	Next Steps

Job Search Tool 17

Phone Script

Calling someone and getting voice mail.

Contact: Hello this is Jan Reisse. I am not available to take your call right now. If you will leave your name, number and a short message, I will be happy to return your call. Thank you.

Caller: Hello Jan, my name is Ron Staple. I can be reached at 436-555-9279. Greg Bates suggested I give you a call, as he thinks it would be beneficial for us to meet. If it is convenient for you, I can be reached on my cell phone at 436-555-9279. If you are not able to call, I will call again in the next few days. Again this is Ron Staple S-T-A-P-L-E, referred to you by Greg Bates. I can be reached at 436-555-9279. Jan, I look forward to meeting with you.

Job Search Tool 18

Networking Meeting Time Allocation

Agenda Item	Total Minutes (20-Minute Meeting)	Total Minutes (30-Minute Meeting)
Introduction, Thanks, and Business Card Exchange	2	2
Transitioning Message and Personal Marketing Message	2	3
Advice on Search and/or Career History	4	6
Networking Contacts	10	15
Follow-Up, Offer of Assistance, and Thank-You	2	4

Job Search Tool 19

Networking Meeting Transition Questions

<u>Transition from *you* talking to *the contact* talking:</u>

1. What would you do if you were in my shoes?
2. What has your career path been?
3. Have you ever been through a transition?
4. What key skills are employers looking for today?
5. What makes the best people in your organization stand out?
6. What is your perception of the current job market?

<u>Transition from advice to your Target List:</u>

1. Do you know any of the people on my Target List?
2. Do you know anyone that works at the companies on my Target List?
3. Can you think of anyone not on my Target List whom I should meet?
4. Is there anyone else in your organization that you think I should meet?
5. What leaders in our community do you admire most, and recommend that I add to my Target List?
6. What companies do you admire, and recommend that I add to my Target List? Do you know anyone at that company?

Job Search Tool 20

Good Listening Skills

✓ Humans think 500 – 600 words per minute, but we talk 100 – 200 words per minute. Stay focused.
✓ Brief verbal acknowledgements let people know you're listening. Say "wow", "interesting", "really", "ok" periodically during the conversation to reinforce your interest.
✓ Nod your head occasionally.
✓ Don't talk. You can't listen while you're talking.
✓ Take notes to keep your mind active and help you stay focused.
✓ Let others finish thoughts and sentences before you respond.
✓ Listen to the content and the intent.
✓ Maintain eye contact, but don't stare.
✓ Have positive body language.
✓ Make sure your facial expressions support your verbal message.
✓ Don't cross your arms; this can be interpreted as negative.
✓ Sitting or standing up straight sends the message that you're actively listening, while slouching says you aren't.
✓ Don't be restless in your chair. Be engaged.
✓ Avoid nervous gestures such as tapping a pen, bouncing your leg, or checking your watch.
✓ Sit where you can clearly see the contact's body language so that you can evaluate it.
✓ Ask questions for clarification.
✓ Rephrase what has been said to demonstrate understanding.

Job Search Tool 21

Requirements vs. Candidate Competency (RCC) Chart

KEITH A. MARTINS

315.606.3759   kamartins@email.net

County Hospital
Assistant Administrator

Operational Management	• Full P/L (sales, operations, finance and HR) for seven businesses in 13 locations.
Aligning Mission, Vision and Values	• Implemented learning map to tell the story describing our future. • Implemented a leadership development program to provide front line feedback to leaders on their behavior supporting the MVV. • Implemented roundtable discussions with all employees to listen and engage them in the business.
Long and short term planning	• Implemented balanced scorecard to clarify critical success factors, current performance and future expectations. • Oversaw development and execution of business plans, revenue growth plans, capital requirements and expense budgets for seven locations.
Human Resources Facilities, Housing Keeping and Security Interaction with Senior Management	• HR division leader for 13 operations • Engineering degree with operating experience • Frequent interaction with Officer level positions
Disciplined	• Myers-Briggs style ISTJ
Business Development	• Implementing plans to shift loyalty of Medical Group to hospital
Performance Improvement	• Procedures costs / procedure less in 2006 than 2005. • Procedure volumes more in 2006 versus 2005

Job Search Tool 22

Interview Checklist

✓ Directions– Verified.
✓ Business Cards.
✓ Agenda
✓ Requirements vs. Competencies Comparison (RCC) Chart– One for each person you will meet, plus extras.
✓ List of Questions– For each person you will meet.
✓ Integration Plan– For the hiring manager.
✓ Resume– Bring extra copies.
✓ Portfolio– For "Show and Tell."
✓ Research on People and Company– Well-organized; not piled in a folder.
✓ Briefcase or Portfolio– For paperwork.
✓ Notepad, Pen, and Extra Pen– For notes.
✓ Watch– To make sure you execute your agenda in the time allotted.
✓ Calendar– In case they want to schedule additional interviews.
✓ PDA– For contact information.
✓ Cell Phone– To call in case of emergency.
✓ References– Do not give a copy unless specifically requested.
✓ Compensation History– Do not give a copy unless specifically requested.
✓ Thank-you Notes– To write before you leave the building.
✓ Breathe Mints
✓ Comb or Hairbrush.
✓ Spare Change– For parking meters.
✓ Money– Small bills for unexpected costs.

Job Search Tool 23

Negotiation List

Benefits
Eligibility for insurance (medical, dental, vision, or life)
401(k) eligibility and vesting period
Pension plan eligibility and vesting period
Early vacation eligibility
Extra vacation
Vacation schedule for future years
Carryover of unused vacation days
Supplemental vacation at key service milestones
Paid holidays
Flexible use of holidays
Personal holidays
Carryover of unused holidays
Tuition reimbursement
Life insurance
Travel insurance
Accidental death insurance
Personal liability insurance

Relocation Expenses
Additional moving expenses
Temporary housing costs
Assistance in selling current home
Mortgage assistance for high housing costs
Assistance in purchasing new home

Job Search Tool 23

Negotiation List

Perks
Club memberships– ongoing expenses and time to participate
Professional organization memberships– ongoing expenses and time to participate
Trade association memberships– ongoing expenses and time to participate
Professional services, such as financial planning and income tax preparation
Paid parking
Office and/or furnishings upgrades
Company car
Financial planning services
Legal planning services

Job Search Tool 24

Relationship Guidelines

Current Relationship	Future Relationship			
	Acquaintance	Associate	Ally	Advocate
Acquaintance	This level of relationship is based as much on chance as investment. If you have not had any contact with this person for more than one year, you should contact them by e-mail or phone just to get caught up.	Frequent (once per quarter) and consistent contact. Start with e-mails to test receptivity, then phone calls with specific purposes, and finally invitations for face-to-face meetings on both a professional and personal basis. You need to have at least two face-to-face meetings within one year, to get to this level of relationship. To build trust, you should offer to provide assistance.	Frequent (once per quarter) and consistent contact for a number of years. Start with e-mails to test receptivity, then phone calls with specific purposes, and finally invitations for face-to-face meetings on both a professional and personal basis. Face-to-face meetings should take place at least twice per year until you reach this level of relationship. To build trust, you should always offer to provide assistance, without a request. When asked for assistance, you must deliver.	Frequent (every other month) and consistent contact for a number of years. Start with e-mails to test receptivity, then phone calls with specific purposes, and finally invitations for face-to-face meetings on both a professional and personal basis. Face-to-face meetings should take place at least twice per year until you reach this level of relationship. To build trust, you should offer assistance and clearly demonstrate your willingness to provide assistance without a request.
Associate	Lack of contact for more than one year will reduce the level of your relationship.	Contact should be made at least twice per year. If you have not seen this person face-to-face for more than one year, schedule a meeting to get caught up.	Frequent (once per quarter) and consistent contact. Start with e-mails to test receptivity, then phone calls with specific purposes, and finally invitations for face-to-face meetings on both a professional and personal basis. You need to have at least two face-to-face meetings within one year to get to this level of relationship. To build trust, you should offer to provide assistance.	Frequent (once per quarter) and consistent contact for a number of years. Start with e-mails to test receptivity, then phone calls with specific purposes, and finally invitations for face-to-face meetings on both a professional and personal basis. Face-to-face meetings should take place at least twice per year until you reach this level of relationship. To build trust, you should offer assistance and clearly demonstrate your willingness to provide assistance without a request.
Ally	Lack of contact for more than two years will reduce the level of your relationship.	Lack of contact for more than one year will reduce the level of your relationship.	Contact should be made at least twice per year. If you have not seen this person face-to-face for more than one year, schedule a meeting to get caught up.	Frequent (once per quarter) and consistent contact. Start with e-mails to test receptivity, then phone calls with specific purposes, and finally invitations for face-to-face meetings on both a professional and personal basis. You will need to have at least two face-to-face meetings to get to this level of relationship, with annual contact at a minimum. To build trust, you should offer assistance and clearly demonstrate your willingness to provide assistance without a request.
Advocate	Lack of contact for more than three years will reduce the level of your relationship.	Lack of contact for more than two years will reduce the level of your relationship.	Lack of contact for more than one year will reduce the level of your relationship.	Some type of contact should be made at least twice per year. If you have not seen this person face-to-face for more than one year, schedule a meeting to get caught up.

PEOPLE HIRE PEOPLE
-*Not Resumes*
Index